Christopher Columbus
and the First Voyages to the New World

General Editor

William H. Goetzmann
Jack S. Blanton, Sr., Chair in History
   University of Texas at Austin

Consulting Editor

Tom D. Crouch
Chairman, Department of Aeronautics
   National Air and Space Museum
   Smithsonian Institution

WORLD EXPLORERS

Christopher Columbus
and the First Voyages to the New World

Stephen C. Dodge

Introductory Essay by Michael Collins

CHELSEA HOUSE PUBLISHERS

New York · Philadelphia

On the cover   Sixteenth-century Portuguese map and portrait of Christopher Columbus, courtesy of Scala/Art Resource.

Chelsea House Publishers
Editor-in-Chief   Remmel Nunn
Managing Editor   Karyn Gullen Browne
Copy Chief   Juliann Barbato
Picture Editor   Adrian G. Allen
Art Director   Maria Epes
Deputy Copy Chief   Mark Rifkin
Series Design   Loraine Machlin
Manufacturing Manager   Gerald Levine
Production Manager   Joseph Romano
Production Coordinator   Marie Claire Cebrián

World Explorers
Senior Editor   Sean Dolan

Staff for CHRISTOPHER COLUMBUS AND
THE FIRST VOYAGES TO THE NEW WORLD
Copy Editor   Philip Koslow
Editorial Assistant   Martin Mooney
Picture Researcher   Alan Gottlieb

3   5   7   9   8   6   4   2

Library of Congress Cataloging-in-Publication Data

Dodge, Steven.
Christopher Columbus and the First Voyages to the New World/
Steven Dodge.
p.   cm.—(World explorers)
Includes bibliographical references.
Summary: Examines the life and times of Christopher Columbus
and describes his voyages to the New World.
ISBN 0-7910-1299-9
        0-7910-1522-X (pbk.)

1. Columbus, Christopher—Juvenile literature.   2. America—
—Discovery and exploration—Spanish—Juvenile literature.
3. Explorers—America—Biography—Juvenile literature.
4. Explorers—Spain—Biography—Juvenile
literature.   [1. Columbus,
Christopher.   2. Explorers.   3. America—Discovery and
exploration—
Spanish.]   I. Title.   II. Series.
E111.D65   1990
970.01′5′092—dc20   90-2059
[B]   CIP
[92]   AC

CONTENTS

WORLD EXPLORERS

THE EARLY EXPLORERS

Herodotus and the Explorers of the Classical Age
Marco Polo and the Medieval Explorers
The Viking Explorers

THE FIRST GREAT AGE OF DISCOVERY

Jacques Cartier, Samuel de Champlain, and the Explorers of Canada
Christopher Columbus and the First Voyages to the New World
From Coronado to Escalante: The Explorers of the Spanish Southwest
Hernando de Soto and the Explorers of the American South
Sir Francis Drake and the Struggle for an Ocean Empire
Vasco da Gama and the Portuguese Explorers
La Salle and the Explorers of the Mississippi
Ferdinand Magellan and the Discovery of the World Ocean
Pizarro, Orellana, and the Exploration of the Amazon
The Search for the Northwest Passage
Giovanni da Verrazano and the Explorers of the Atlantic Coast

THE SECOND GREAT AGE OF DISCOVERY

Roald Amundsen and the Quest for the South Pole
Daniel Boone and the Opening of the Ohio Country
Captain James Cook and the Explorers of the Pacific
The Explorers of Alaska
John Charles Frémont and the Great Western Reconnaissance
Alexander von Humboldt, Colossus of Exploration
Lewis and Clark and the Route to the Pacific
Alexander Mackenzie and the Explorers of Canada
Robert Peary and the Quest for the North Pole
Zebulon Pike and the Explorers of the American Southwest
John Wesley Powell and the Great Surveys of the American West
Jedediah Smith and the Mountain Men of the American West
Henry Stanley and the European Explorers of Africa
Lt. Charles Wilkes and the Great U.S. Exploring Expedition

THE THIRD GREAT AGE OF DISCOVERY

Apollo to the Moon
The Explorers of the Undersea World
The First Men in Space
The Mission to Mars and Beyond
Probing Deep Space

CHELSEA HOUSE PUBLISHERS

Into the Unknown

Michael Collins

It is difficult to define most eras in history with any precision, but not so the space age. On October 4, 1957, it burst on us with little warning when the Soviet Union launched *Sputnik*, a 184-pound cannonball that circled the globe once every 96 minutes. Less than 4 years later, the Soviets followed this first primitive satellite with the flight of Yuri Gagarin, a 27-year-old fighter pilot who became the first human to orbit the earth. The Soviet Union's success prompted President John F. Kennedy to decide that the United States should "land a man on the moon and return him safely to earth" before the end of the 1960s. We now had not only a space age but a space race.

I was born in 1930, exactly the right time to allow me to participate in Project Apollo, as the U.S. lunar program came to be known. As a young man growing up, I often found myself too young to do the things I wanted—or suddenly too old, as if someone had turned a switch at midnight. But for Apollo, 1930 was the perfect year to be born, and I was very lucky. In 1966 I enjoyed circling the earth for three days, and in 1969 I flew to the moon and laughed at the sight of the tiny earth, which I could cover with my thumbnail.

How the early explorers would have loved the view from space! With one glance Christopher Columbus could have plotted his course and reassured his crew that the world was indeed round. In 90 minutes Magellan could have looked down at every port of call in the *Victoria's* three-year circumnavigation of the globe. Given a chance to map their route from orbit, Lewis and Clark could have told President Jefferson that there was no easy Northwest Passage but that a continent of exquisite diversity awaited their scrutiny.

In a physical sense, we have already gone to most places that we can. That is not to say that there are not new adventures awaiting us deep in the sea or on the red plains of Mars, but more important than reaching new places will be understanding those we have already visited. There are vital gaps in our understanding of how our planet works as an ecosystem and how our planet fits into the infinite order of the universe. The next great age may well be the age of assimilation, in which we use microscope and telescope to evaluate what we have discovered and put that knowledge to use. The adventure of being first to reach may be replaced by the satisfaction of being first to grasp. Surely that is a form of exploration as vital to our well-being, and perhaps even survival, as the distinction of being the first to explore a specific geographical area.

The explorers whose stories are told in the books of this series did not just sail perilous seas, scale rugged mountains, traverse blistering deserts, dive to the depths of the ocean, or land on the moon. Their voyages and expeditions were journeys of mind as much as of time and distance, through which they—and all of mankind—were able to reach a greater understanding of our universe. That challenge remains, for all of us. The imperative is to see, to understand, to develop knowledge that others can use, to help nurture this planet that sustains us all. Perhaps being born in 1975 will be as lucky for a new generation of explorer as being born in 1930 was for Neil Armstrong, Buzz Aldrin, and Mike Collins.

The Reader's Journey

William H. Goetzmann

This volume is one of a series that takes us with the great explorers of the ages on bold journeys over the oceans and the continents and into outer space. As we travel along with these imaginative and courageous journeyers, we share their adventures and their knowledge. We also get a glimpse of that mysterious and inextinguishable fire that burned in the breast of men such as Magellan and Columbus—the fire that has propelled all those throughout the ages who have been driven to leave behind family and friends for a voyage into the unknown.

No one has ever satisfactorily explained the urge to explore, the drive to go to the "back of beyond." It is certain that it has been present in man almost since he began walking erect and first ventured across the African savannas. Sparks from that same fire fueled the transoceanic explorers of the Ice Age, who led their people across the vast plain that formed a land bridge between Asia and North America, and the astronauts and scientists who determined that man must reach the moon.

Besides an element of adventure, all exploration involves an element of mystery. We must not confuse exploration with discovery. Exploration is a purposeful human activity—a search for something. Discovery may be the end result of that search; it may also be an accident, as when Columbus found a whole new world while searching for the Indies. Often, the explorer may not even realize the full significance of what he has discovered, as was the case with Columbus. Exploration, on the other hand, is the product of a cultural or individual curiosity; it is a unique process that has enabled mankind to know and understand the world's oceans, continents, and polar regions. It is at the heart of scientific thinking. One of its most significant aspects is that it teaches people to ask the right questions; by doing so, it forces us to reevaluate what we think we know and understand. Thus knowledge progresses, and we are driven constantly to a new awareness and appreciation of the universe in all its infinite variety.

The motivation for exploration is not always pure. In his fascination with the new, man often forgets that others have been there before him. For example, the popular notion of the discovery of America overlooks the complex Indian civilizations that had existed there for thousands of years before the arrival of Europeans. Man's desire for conquest, riches, and fame is often linked inextricably with his quest for the unknown, but a story that touches so closely on the human essence must of necessity treat war as well as peace, avarice with generosity, both pride and humility, frailty and greatness. The story of exploration is above all a story of humanity and of man's understanding of his place in the universe.

The WORLD EXPLORERS series has been divided into four sections. The first treats the explorers of the ancient world, the Viking explorers of the 9th through the 11th centuries, and Marco Polo and the medieval explorers. The rest of the series is divided into three great ages of exploration. The first is the era of Columbus and Magellan: the period spanning the 15th and 16th centuries, which saw the discovery and exploration of the New World and the world ocean. The second might be called the age of science and imperialism, the era made possible by the scientific advances of the 17th century, which witnessed the discovery of the world's last two undiscovered continents, Australia and Antarctica, the mapping of all the continents and oceans, and the establishment of colonies all over the world. The third great age refers to the most ambitious quests of the 20th century—the probing of space and of the ocean's depths.

As we reach out into the darkness of outer space and other galaxies, we come to better understand how our ancestors confronted *oecumene,* or the vast earthly unknown. We learn once again the meaning of an unknown 18th-century sea captain's advice to navigators:

> And if by chance you make a landfall on the shores of another sea in a far country inhabited by savages and barbarians, remember you this: the greatest danger and the surest hope lies not with fires and arrows but in the quicksilver hearts of men.

At its core, exploration is a series of moral dramas. But it is these dramas, involving new lands, new people, and exotic ecosystems of staggering beauty, that make the explorers' stories not only moral tales but also some of the greatest adventure stories ever recorded. They represent the process of learning in its most expansive and vivid forms. We see that real life, past and present, transcends even the adventures of the starship *Enterprise.*

Where Gold Is Born

The year 1492 was a momentous one for the nation of Spain, a kingdom recently unified through the marriage of its reigning monarchs, Ferdinand and Isabella, and their zeal in bringing together the many disparate elements of their common fiefdom. On the second day of that year, Sultan Muhammad XI, whom the Spanish called Boabdil, rode out from the besieged Moorish city of Granada, in southern Spain, and offered his surrender to Ferdinand and Isabella. Granada's capitulation brought to an end more than 750 years of warfare between the Spanish and the Moors, North African practitioners of Islam who had conquered all of Spain in the 8th century. The Reconquista, as Catholic Spain's war with the Moors was known, had proceeded steadily but slowly ever since, but the defeat of Boabdil meant the end of the last Moorish stronghold in Spain. When los Reyes Católicos (the Catholic Monarchs, an honorary title that would be bestowed on Ferdinand and Isabella by a grateful papacy) seated themselves in the throne room in the Alhambra, the legendary palace of Granada's Moorish rulers, on that January day in 1492, it seemed that their dream of ruling over a unified, Catholic Spain had at last been fulfilled.

Other auguries of greatness were to follow. Later that year, a scholar named Elio Antonio de Nebrija, a linguist, theologian, jurist, and grammarian hailed as "the light of Salamanca" (a city in west-central Spain whose famed

A 1493 Italian woodcut shows a benevolent Ferdinand, king of Spain, witnessing Columbus's discovery of the New World. News of Columbus reaching "the Indies" created a sensation in Italy, where multiple editions of his letter on the expedition were printed and sold.

university attracted scholars from around the world), completed and published his *Art of the Castilian Language*. Dedicated to the devout Isabella, the book was the first grammar of a modern European language, but the pious queen, upon being presented with a copy, wondered at its usefulness for monarchs. "Your Royal Majesty," a member of her court advised, in words that would come to seem prophetic, "language has always been the companion of empire."

Ambitious words, some would even say foolishly optimistic as concerned the court language of a nation only recently united. And perhaps only the most starry-eyed dreamer would have connected them with the departure on August 2, from the small port city of Palos, in southern Spain near the Portugal border, of three small ships: two *caravels*—called the *Niña* and the *Pinta*—and a scarcely larger vessel, a *nao* called the *Santa María*. Certainly, the

This bas-relief, an altarpiece from the cathedral at Granada, depicts Ferdinand and his queen, Isabella, leading their troops into the defeated Moorish capital on January 2, 1492, a date a contemporary historian called the "most distinguished and blessed day there has ever been in Spain."

purpose of the expedition—to reach the Indies (a catchall term used imprecisely to designate the rich Asian regions whence originated the spices, precious metals, and gems coveted by Europe's monarchs and merchants) by sailing west across the broad Atlantic, or Ocean Sea, as it was then known, a route never before attempted—was ambitious enough, but few thought seriously that it would succeed. Ferdinand and Isabella had agreed to sponsor the mission, but only after years of deliberation, and even then not because they believed that it would reach the Indies but because the potential return, should the seemingly impossible occur, made the likely loss of their initially small investment a risk well worth taking. Indeed, the venture was regarded as so dubious that in order to man the ships, the monarchs had deemed it necessary to offer

No eyewitness representations of the Niña, *the* Pinta, *or the* Santa María *exist, but this 1496 Spanish woodcut gives a contemporary artist's view of the type of ship that carried Columbus to the New World.*

a full pardon for any felon willing to serve as a member of the crew. Even the departure point spoke to the lack of importance, in comparison with other matters of state, that the expedition occupied. The tiny fleet was unable to leave from Cádiz, Spain's most important port on the Atlantic, because that city's harbor was filled to overflowing with ships carrying Jewish refugees into exile. In their desire to establish Spain as a Catholic kingdom, Ferdinand and Isabella had decreed that by August 2, 1492, all the nation's Jews had either to convert to Christianity or leave Spain. The penalty for failure to comply was death.

If it is true that only the most visionary dreamer could have foreseen the fulfillment of the words of that now obscure courtier in the departure of those three ships from Palos, it is equally accurate that the person in command of that expedition was such an individual. Christopher Columbus, the silent, stubborn Genoan who had convinced Ferdinand and Isabella to sponsor the voyage and promise him the title of Admiral of the Ocean Sea—a title as grandiose as his ambition—had nurtured his dream through years of obscurity, poverty, mockery, and neglect, sustained only by his unshakable belief that he had been chosen to accomplish what everyone else said was impossible: to sail west across the Ocean Sea in order to reach the East, the fabled Indies, where lay Cathay (China), Cipango (Japan), and India. Of all those involved with the Enterprise of the Indies, as the expedition was known, it was Columbus alone who actually believed that the voyage would be successfully completed, yielding to Ferdinand and Isabella a lucrative overseas empire and to himself riches and glory beyond compare. Equally important, the fanatically devout Columbus believed, would be the spiritual benefits to be reaped by monarch and mariner, for in the Indies would be found hundreds of thousands of souls that could be converted to Christianity, and some of the riches gained could be used to fund a new crusade designed to free the Holy Land from its Muslim captors.

That the exact manner in which the courtier's prophetic utterance would be fulfilled differed greatly from what Columbus had imagined does not lessen the magnitude of his vision or the scale of his accomplishments, for it is in his fidelity to his own dream that Columbus's greatness lies.

But some two months into the voyage, even Columbus must have begun to entertain some doubts. The date had passed by which he had calculated that the fleet would make land at Cipango, and the crew, skeptical to begin with, was bordering on mutiny. Even auspicious signs, such as the prevalence of favorable winds that had carried

This early-16th-century map illustrates the rather fanciful notions held by Europeans regarding the geography and inhabitants of the lands Columbus believed he would reach on his Enterprise of the Indies. Cipango (Zipangri) is the island at left; the mainland supposedly represents both China and India. According to the illustrations, among the things to be found there were elephants, headhunters, pygmies, a Christian monarch, and at lower right, protected by an ornate canopy, a powerful ruler known as the Grand Khan.

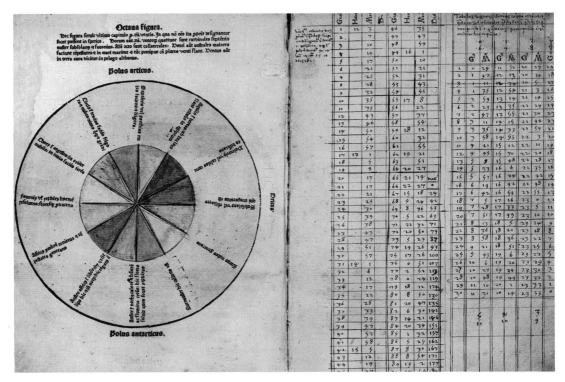

Columbus's handwritten annotations can be seen just to the right of center, next to the wind charts in his copy of Imago Mundi, *a compendium of geographic knowledge that he carried with him to the New World. Columbus also colored in the inner circle of the compass at left, and the margins of virtually every page in the volume are filled with his extensive notations.*

the fleet across the ocean at an unexpectedly rapid clip, were interpreted by the weary and frightened sailors as inauspicious omens. If an easterly wind constantly blew, the crew argued, how then would the sailing ships be able to return to Spain? Columbus's theory about opposing winds at different latitudes left them unconvinced, for they knew, as did everyone but the admiral himself, that his words could be nothing more than conjecture. On October 6, a conference of the ships' officers was held aboard the *Santa María*. The majority of the officers were opposed to venturing any farther into the unknown, but Columbus remained firm, stating that "it was useless to complain, since he had made up his mind to sail to the Indies and intended to continue the voyage until, God willing, he should reach them." (The log that Columbus kept of his journey has disappeared, but 2 of his 16th-century biographers, his youngest son, Ferdinand, and Bartolomé de

Las Casas, made transcriptions of it, which they used in their work. Much of our knowledge of the events of the voyage comes from those sources. Other contemporary or nearly contemporary recountings that make use of eye-witness testimony include the work of the 16th-century historian Gonzalo Fernández de Oviedo, who compiled the first official account of the voyage.) Columbus did, however, concede that if land was not sighted within a few days, he would order the ships to turn back. The fleet sailed on, ever westward, away from all that was known. A couple of days later, large flocks of birds were spotted overhead. Birds were considered sure signs that land was near, so Martín Alonso Pinzón, captain of the *Pinta*, per-suaded Columbus to alter his course slightly to the south-west, in the direction the winged harbingers were flying. Several more days passed, and the crew grew increasingly vocal in their demands that Columbus fulfill his words and turn back. According to Ferdinand Columbus:

> They met together in the holds of the ships, saying that the admiral in his mad fantasy proposed to make himself a lord at the cost of their lives or die in the attempt; that they had already tempted fortune as much as their duty required and had sailed farther from land than any others had done. If the admiral would not turn back, they should heave him overboard and report in Spain that he had fallen in accidentally while observing the stars; and none would question their story.

On the night of October 11, at about 10 o'clock, as all hands on duty scanned the horizon, the captain-general (Columbus's title until he actually discovered something) reported seeing a light on the horizon "like a little wax candle whose flame went up and down." One other sailor reported seeing the same thing, but when several hours passed with no sign of land, the disgruntled crew dismissed it as an optical illusion or a creation of their commander's disordered mind. Finally, at two o'clock the following

When the fleet did not sight land by the date Columbus said it would, his crew threatened to mutiny unless he turned the ships around and returned to Spain, but Columbus told the fearful sailors that if they wished to change course, they would have to cut his head off first.

morning, Rodrigo de Triana, a lookout on the *Pinta*, sang out frantically—"Land! Land!" Pinzón, confirming the sighting, ordered the ship's guns to be fired, the prearranged signal that land had been found. Aboard the three ships, which were sailing close together, the overjoyed sailors sank to their knees and offered thanks to God. Some wept. Soon, all claimed to be able to see, glistening in the moonlight not far off, a sandy beach and the shadows cast by a high bluff. Columbus prudently ordered the ships to stay out of the shallow water near shore until daybreak. The sky began to lighten at about five o'clock, revealing that the beach was protected by dangerous coral reefs, making it impossible for the Spaniards to land. At the captain-general's orders, the ships began to circle in a westward direction. This reconnaissance made it plain that what the mariners had discovered was merely a very small island, not a province of Cipango or Cathay, but their enthusiasm was lessened not a bit. Columbus was certain that the island was only 1 of the more than 7,000 that Marco Polo had asserted lay just off the mainland of China. (Polo was a 13th-century Venetian traveler whose accounts of his adventures provided educated Europeans with much of what little they knew about the Orient.)

At around noon, a placid bay, suitable for a landing, was found, and the impatient men prepared to disembark. In the tropical sunshine, the shoreline was clearly revealed—a pristine, gleaming beach, backed with trees, of a kind unfamiliar to the Europeans, with bright green foliage, in the branches of which jabbered monkeys and parrots. A couple of pelicans walked across the sand. The forest also hid the island's native inhabitants, an apparently gentle, peace-loving people known as the Taino, of the Arawakan language group. Their initial hesitation gave way to curiosity, and the Indians soon left their cover and "all came down to the beach, shouting." In his play about Columbus, *El Nuevo Mundo* (The New World), Lope de

Vega, the great Spanish writer of the 16th and 17th centuries often hailed as the father of modern drama, portrays the Indians exclaiming in wonder about the great ships in the bay, the likes of which they had obviously never seen before, "There are three houses on the water!" Columbus had his own interpretation—he believed that the Indians were engaged, as were the white men, in "giving thanks to God."

Three launches were lowered, one from each ship, and the Europeans made for shore. Surrounded by his officers, Columbus kneeled and kissed the earth of the New World, planted the royal flag of Ferdinand and Isabella and the banner of the expedition, which was emblazoned with a green cross, and officially took possession of the island, the nearby regions, and their people for Spain. The island, he proclaimed, would be named San Salvador (Holy Savior) "in honor of God, who had pointed it out to him, and saved him from many dangers," as Ferdinand Columbus put it.

Having observed from a respectful distance this curious ceremony, the Indians now approached closer. Las Casas described the epic first encounter:

> The Indians, of whom there were a large number, gazed dumbstruck at the Christians, looking with wonder at their beards, their clothes, and the whiteness of their skin. They directed their attentions toward the men with beards, but especially toward the admiral, who they realized was the most important of the group, either from his imposing physical presence or from his scarlet clothing. They touched the men's beards with their fingers and carefully examined the paleness of their hands and faces. Seeing that they were innocent, the admiral and his men did not resist their actions.

Columbus and the Spaniards were equally astounded by the Indians. In his log, Columbus wrote that the Indians

A 16th-century engraving of Columbus coming ashore at San Salvador. In 1926, Watlings Island, a tiny body of land some 350 miles southeast of Miami, Florida, changed its name to San Salvador in the belief that Columbus made his first landfall there. Although the issue is still disputed, most historians believe that Watlings is indeed Columbus's San Salvador.

all went "quite naked as their mothers bore them," even the women. He found the men "to be very well-built, of very handsome bodies and very fine faces; the hair coarse, almost like the brow of a horse's tail, and short, the hair they wear over the eyebrows, except for a hank behind that they wear long and never cut."

What amazed the Europeans, particularly Columbus, even more than the Indians' appearance was their seeming innocence. In the report of the expedition that he submitted to Ferdinand and Isabella, Columbus described them as "wonderfully timorous," unwilling to use weapons because they are "timid beyond cure." He added:

They are so artless and so free with all they possess, that no one would believe it without having seen it. Of anything they have, if you ask them for it, they never say no; rather they invite the person to share it, and show as much love as if they were giving their hearts; and whether the thing be of value or of small price, at once they are content with whatever little thing of whatever kind may be given to them.

Columbus had good reason to admire this last quality—generosity in trade—for before leaving Spain the ships had been stocked with plenty of glass pearls, cheap mirrors, colored beads, and small bells, which the adventurers intended to trade for gold with the presumably unsophisticated inhabitants of the Indies. Although he recognized that the Indians possessed "a very keen intelligence," their lack of aggression suggested to him "that with 50 armed men these people could be brought under control and made to do whatever one might wish." "Christendom will do good business with these Indians," wrote Columbus in his log, "especially Spain, whose subjects they must all become." Thus, soon after a peaceful meeting on a tranquil beach—an encounter that might truly be described as earth shattering in that it forever changed man's conception of his world—was born the germ of the idea that would spell tragedy for the native inhabitants of the New World.

For the moment, however, all remained peaceful. Despite the excitement of having found land, Columbus was eager to sail on. San Salvador was only a small island whose inhabitants were poor, with no access to precious metals. Not far off, Columbus was sure, was Cathay, where Marco Polo said the palaces had roofs of gold. That evening, the Europeans returned to their ships, taking with them as captives six of the Indians. In the morning, they weighed anchor and moved on, in search of, in Columbus's words, "the place where gold is born."

A Noble and Powerful City

Sometime between August and October 1451, Susanna Colombo, formerly di Fontanarossa, wife of Domenico, a wool weaver and tavern keeper, gave birth to her first child, a boy. His parents named him Cristoforo, after St. Christopher, who according to Christian tradition carried the Christ Child across a dangerous river on his shoulders and has since been revered as the patron saint of travelers. (Christopher is the English equivalent of the intrepid mariner's given name; Columbus is derived from the Latin version of his surname. It is used in English because his fame was first widely circulated in a history written in Latin by Pietro Martire d'Anghiera, a diplomat and humanist who was in residence at the Spanish court at Barcelona when Columbus made his triumphant return from his first voyage. To the Spanish, Columbus was and is known as Cristóbal Colón.)

Domenico and Susanna made their home in Genoa, "that noble and powerful city on the sea," as Columbus was later to refer to it. Although its nobility is a matter of subjective judgment, there can be no denying that during Columbus's childhood Genoa was powerful. Located in northwest Italy on the Ligurian Sea, Genoa was ideally situated to trade on the Mediterranean, the sea separating southern Europe from northern Africa and linking both those areas to the Levant, as the region at its eastern end (modern-day Turkey, Syria, Lebanon, and Israel) was

The teeming harbor of Genoa, the prosperous seaport on Italy's Ligurian coast where Columbus was born in 1451. This painting was done in 1481 and depicts a Genoese fleet readying itself for action against the Turks, who then controlled much of the eastern Mediterranean.

known. At the time, the Mediterranean was Europe's commercial lifeline; it represented, to most Europeans, the literal center of the known world. Even the most educated scholars of the day admitted the existence of only three continents—Asia, Africa, and Europe—surrounded by a great body of water, the Ocean Sea. At the very center of what Europeans considered the known world was the Mediterranean, which permitted Europeans as much contact as they deemed necessary with the mysterious regions of Africa and Asia, most importantly by allowing maritime entrepreneurs from city-states such as Genoa and Venice (Genoa's great rival on the Italian peninsula) access to the treasures of the East. These items—silk, cotton, gold, silver, and "spices": cinnamon, pepper, nutmeg, cloves, mace, incense, sandalwood, resin, coffee, tea, sugar, various herbs used to make perfume and medicine—reached

A 15th-century artistic representation of Jerusalem. Medieval cartographers placed Jerusalem at the center of the known world. Regarded as a holy city by Christians, Muslims, and Jews, in Columbus's day Jerusalem figured prominently in various European schemes to free the Holy Land from Muslim control, plans whose success would serve the added purpose of reopening the Levant to European spice merchants.

the savvy traders of the Levant via a long, tortuous sea and overland trade route from their places of origin in India, Ceylon, the Spice Islands, and even China, regions referred to collectively by Europeans as the Indies. From the Levant, these goods were carried in European ships back to Genoa, Venice, and other cities, where merchants and bankers arranged for their further distribution across the continent.

During Columbus's childhood, Genoa and Venice were the two most important maritime centers on the "most hospitable sea of the globe," as Europeans regarded the Mediterranean. Genoa's mapmakers were highly regarded, particularly for their *portolanos*, as the compact, portable guides to the Mediterranean's harbors were known, and between them, the Genoese and the Venetians divided most of the sea's islands and controlled virtually all trade

(continued on page 30)

The Venetian adventurer Marco Polo arrives at the court of the Mongol emperor Kublai Khan in an illustration from a 1375 edition of The Description of the World, *Polo's ghostwritten account of his journeys. Polo's wanderings took him more than 20,000 miles over 24 years; his description of the splendor and wonders of the East stimulated the imagination of medieval Europe, but he claimed that he had not written even half of what he had seen.*

IRELAND
Dublin

ENGLAND
London

IRELAND

Rhine
River

Cologne

Nuremburg

K

Seine River

Paris

Vienna

Rhone River

Milan

Venice

Genoa

NAVARRE

LIGURIAN
SEA

Pisa

ADRIATIC SE

PORTUGAL

CASTILE

ARAGON

I T A L Y

Lisbon

Barcelona

Corsica

Rome

Lagos

Cádiz

GRANADA

Sardinia

M E D I T E R R A N E
E

NORTH AFRICA

Sicily

Map of the Mediterranean World

N

Danube *River*

B L A C K   S E A

Constantinople

A E G E A N

Chios

S E A

S E A

The Mediterranean Sea and surrounding regions in the mid-15th century, around the time of Columbus's birth.

Spices were among the wonders that Polo described and Europeans coveted. This illustration of a pepper harvest on Madagascar comes from the 1375 edition of Polo's book.

(continued from page 27)

between East and West. Venetian traders dominated the commerce with Egypt in pepper, and Genoese mariners maintained such a powerful presence in the Middle East that the Black Sea was sometimes referred to as "Genoa's lake." The dominance of these two cities was of long standing, as was their rivalry—the Venetian Marco Polo had dictated his account of his fantastic adventures in the Orient while languishing in a Genoese jail after being taken as a prisoner of war in an epic naval battle between the two powers—but events were transpiring that would forever change the Mediterranean world.

In 1453, the year Columbus celebrated his second birthday, the city of Constantinople (known today as Istanbul) fell to the Ottoman Turks, and with it went most of the Levant. The loss of Constantinople—the capital of the Eastern Roman Empire, the second city of Christendom, the gateway to the East for Mediterranean Europe—was a devastating blow for Genoa and Venice. The Turks, the seven-hilled city's conquerors, were Muslims, as believers in the religion of Islam are known; their ships soon became the scourge of the eastern Mediterranean, and their land forces ultimately overran the Balkan Peninsula and rampaged as far north on the European continent as Vienna. Souls as well as territory were at stake in the warfare between Christian Europe and the Ottoman Empire. Muslims and Christians regarded each other as infidels, or unbelievers, and in an age in which religion dominated virtually every aspect of daily life, their struggle naturally took on a sacred as well as a secular dimension. In Genoa, the news that Constantinople had fallen, which arrived in early July 1453, was greeted as nothing less than a catastrophe. The message sent by Angelo Lomellino, administrator of the Genoese district of Constantinople, was succinct in its appraisal of the situation: "No longer will our ships be able to sail toward the Black Sea bearing our goods. The certificates of the trading companies are henceforth worthless."

Merchants often value pragmatism as a supreme virtue, and both Genoa and Venice quickly began to examine ways to adjust. With a closer proximity to the Ottoman strongholds and a stronger military than Genoa, Venice pursued a policy of accommodation, seeking common ground on which to build mutually beneficial commercial arrangements with the Turks, defying the pope's edict forbidding intercourse with the infidel. (This policy earned Venice the enmity of other Catholic states, many of whom united against it in the early 16th century, as well as sanctions by the Church.) Located on the opposite side of the Italian peninsula, Genoa adopted a different tactic and sought ways to invest the wealth it had earned over the years. With the East closed to it, Genoa naturally looked west. Its bankers and entrepreneurs began to invest capital in Seville, Barcelona, Lisbon, and elsewhere, and soon

Genoese communities were to be found in many cities in Spain and Portugal. Some 100 years after the fall of Constantinople, the ingenuity of Genoese capitalists enabled the city to enjoy a rebirth as one of Europe's financial centers.

But during Columbus's childhood Genoa's capitalist reincarnation was far off, and the fortunes of the Colombo family more closely reflected the uncertainty of Genoa's more immediate future. As a young married man, Domenico Colombo prospered. He rose from apprentice to proprietor of his own business and became a member of the wool weavers' guild, and he and his bride were able to rent a house and some property near the wall that marked the outskirts of the city proper. Politically connected, he received an appointment to be gatekeeper, which added to both his social standing and his income, but within Genoa, as in many of Italy's cities, it was a time of factional strife. Domenico was a supporter of the

Venice, Genoa's great rival in the Mediterranean, is built on 118 tiny islands in the midst of a lagoon. The islands are connected by a series of bridges and canals. Venice's control of the spice trade made it the envy of Europe, inspiring jealous princes and merchants to seek an alternate route to the Indies.

Fregoso family, who were themselves allied, in the treacherous and seemingly unending struggle for political power in Italy between the papacy and the Holy Roman Empire, with the Guelphs, the papal party. When the Fregosos were driven from power by the opposition faction, Domenico lost his sinecure, and his business suffered as well. The family was forced to move. Eventually, Domenico resorted to running a tavern in an attempt to meet his financial responsibilities, but he was jailed on at least one occasion for failure to pay his debts.

Hard times meant that there was little opportunity for Domenico's red-haired oldest son to obtain an education, for he was needed to help out with the family business. Ferdinand Columbus later claimed that his father attended college in Italy, but more reliable evidence indicates that Columbus received little or no formal education, and it is almost certain that he reached adulthood virtually illiterate. By his teenage years, Columbus was already accomplished at carding wool, as the process of combing, or straightening, raw wool fibers before spinning or twisting them into thread is known, but he disliked the tedious work in his father's shop. As a Genoan, he could not help but be exposed to the various facets of the maritime life, and even as a young boy his mind was already on the sea. He wrote Ferdinand and Isabella in later years that he "entered upon the sea sailing" at a "very tender age" and claimed at another point to have made his first voyage at age 10.

Specifics aside, it is clear that by his adolescence Columbus was making regular Mediterranean journeys, most likely first on short jaunts aboard the ships of family friends with consignments of his father's merchandise, then on longer trips as a crewman aboard vessels owned by the Centurions, Spinolas, and DiNegros, three of Genoa's most prominent shipbuilding families. While ashore, he continued to help out in the wool shop, but it was soon apparent to all that his chosen destiny was the sea. In 1473 or thereabouts, Columbus sailed aboard the 3-masted *Roxana*, named after a beautiful Ligurian woman who had been kidnapped by Turkish pirates, some 900 miles to the island of Chios, which alone among the islands of the eastern Mediterranean had succeeded in maintaining its economic ties to Genoa. He remained on the island for about a year, savoring his first taste of genuine independence. Ferdinand Columbus claimed that sometime during this same period Columbus served as commander of a warship belonging to Duke René of Anjou. His mission was supposedly to have been to engage in acts of piracy against the king of Aragon, but it is unlikely that such a young, relatively unknown sailor would have been given a position of command. Columbus was building a reputation for himself as a reliable seaman and merchant—with his help, Domenico was able to raise himself out of debt—but he was not yet sufficiently well known to be entrusted with a captainship.

In August 1476 occurred one of the turning points of Columbus's life. That month, he shipped out with a convoy of five Genoese ships laden with goods for sale in Flanders and England. The proposed journey was the longest on which Columbus had yet embarked, and it offered the 25-year-old adventurer his first opportunity to brave the waters of the Ocean Sea. Not long after the vessels passed through the Strait of Gibraltar and thereby from the Mediterranean into the Atlantic, they were set upon by a fleet of 13 pirate ships commanded by the notorious French buccaneer Guillaume de Casenove. The battle in the waters off Cape St. Vincent raged all day. When the French ships drew near enough to attempt to board the Genoese vessels, the desperate sailors attempted to rebuff them by launching pots of blazing pitch at their decks and rigging, but by this point the ships were too close together for such a maneuver to be successful. The French ships did indeed catch fire, but the flames soon spread to the merchant vessels as well. By nightfall, four pirate ships had gone down, as had three of the vessels of the Genoese, carrying with them to the bottom of the ocean so many men that it was said that back home "the women ma[d]e a world of their tears." Columbus's ship, the *Bechalla*, was among those that sank. Although he had been wounded, he survived, "by miracle," according to his own account, and in his son and biographer's words, "because he was a prodigious swimmer." Seizing hold of an oar or some drifting wreckage, he spent the night swimming the six miles to shore. Near morning, utterly spent, he washed up on the beach near Lagos, a fishing village on Portugal's southern coast, a rugged region known as the Algarve. Some of the town's residents found him there, took him in, treated him with great charity, and nursed him back to health. After several weeks of convalescence, he resolved to make his way to Lisbon, Portugal's greatest city, where his brother Bartholomeo had established himself in business as a cartographer.

A wool weaver at work, from an illustrated 16th-century manuscript. With his eyes fixed firmly on the sea from a young age, Columbus had little patience for his father's trade, and he left it behind as soon as he was able.

The Crown upon the Head

It is hard to imagine a more propitious place for an ambitious, imaginative mariner like Christopher Columbus to find himself than Lisbon in the 1470s. The Turkish conquest of the Levant was just one in a series of events that would over time transfer power in Europe from those states that controlled the Mediterranean to those that ruled the oceans. In the forefront of that transition was Portugal. Wrote the nation's greatest poet, Luiz de Camões, author of *The Lusiads*, an epic recounting of Portuguese history, in particular the exploits of its brave seafaring men: "If Spain is the head of Europe, Portugal, where land ends and sea begins, is the crown upon the head." Portugal being the westernmost of the nations of the European continent, its entire coastline is on the Atlantic Ocean. Its greatest city, Lisbon, is built on seven hills, like Rome and Constantinople; Lisbon's harbor, on the broad mouth of the Tagus River, just a few miles upriver from the Atlantic, was one of the best in Europe. Goods from around the world were unloaded at its bustling wharves and quays, and ships from every country in Europe called there.

More than any other nation in Europe, Portugal was engaged in the business of exploration. Even before Constantinople's fall to the Turks, the Portuguese were seeking new trade routes, new ways to avail themselves of the wealth of the East. This interest in exploration came about

Christopher Columbus as a young man. Columbus was never drawn or painted from life, which accounts for the many different ways in which he has been portrayed. Those who knew Columbus described him as being taller than average, with blue eyes, freckles, and reddish hair that went gray and then white at a young age.

largely through the impetus of one man, Prince Henry, known as the Navigator, the third son of the Portuguese monarch João I.

As was true of so many individuals of the day, faith was what drove Henry. As a young man and again at other times throughout his life, Henry was a warrior, pushing Portugal's struggle against the Moors, who had conquered his homeland as well as Spain. In 1415, at the age of 21, Henry distinguished himself at the head of Portuguese forces that overran the Moorish stronghold at Ceuta, a trading center in North Africa just across the Strait of Gibraltar. The riches the Portuguese found there—gold, silver, pepper, cinnamon, cloves, and ginger—stimulated Henry's imagination, leaving him determined to find for Portugal a means to directly obtain such treasures.

Thus began his life's work. Henry retired from the royal court and retreated to Sagres, a promontory in the Algarve between Lagos and Cape St. Vincent that overlooks the Atlantic. There, almost 200 feet above the rough waves of the ocean, this prince, of whom it had been foretold at his birth that he "was bound to engage in great and noble conquests, and above all was he bound to attempt the

Lisbon, the great Portuguese city where Columbus joined his brother Bartholomeo in 1476. The exploits of Portugal's adventurous mariners gradually led to a shift in political and economic power in Europe away from Mediterranean cities to nations with more far-flung economic enterprises.

discovery of things which were hidden from other men, and secret," constructed a school of navigation, an observatory, a church and chapel, and a palace. From Sagres, the pious Navigator—he was a lifelong celibate and wore a hair shirt each of his days as penance for his failings—sponsored and dispatched a series of expeditions south in the Atlantic along Africa's west coast. His contemporary and biographer, Gomes Eanes de Zurara, described what Henry hoped these missions would accomplish: "To discover what lay beyond the Canaries and Cape Bojador; to trade with any Christians who might dwell in the lands beyond; to discover the extent of the Mohammedan [Muslim] dominions; to find a Christian king who would help him to fight the infidel; to spread the Christian faith; to fulfill the prescriptions of his horoscope, which bound him to engage in great and noble conquests and attempt the discovery of things that were hidden from other men; to find Guinea."

Gold, God, and glory; these were the objectives that inspired Henry, as they would obsess Columbus. Guinea, where the bulge of the African continent falls away to the east, was said to be the source of the gold that had filled the countinghouses of Ceuta. Europeans knew that spices, which because of their value as flavor enhancers and preservatives were almost as sought after as gems or precious metals, came from the Orient, but Henry believed that his mariners might be able to find another trade route to the East. His mariners were also instructed to search for evidence of Prester John, an apocryphal monarch believed to rule over a Christian kingdom somewhere in the midst of the Muslim infidels. Europeans had been hearing about Prester John since at least 1165, when a letter supposedly written by that potentate surfaced at Constantinople at the court of Manuel Comnenus, ruler of the Eastern Roman Empire. In the missive, Prester John promised his aid to Christian Europe in its struggle with the Muslims and boasted that he reigned supreme, "exceed[ing] in riches,

Henry the Navigator, the pious prince whose encouragement of exploration helped make tiny Portugal one of the most powerful nations of Europe. The young man at lower right would become King João II of Portugal in 1481. A canny, ruthless politician and a generous patron of Renaissance culture and science, João II, known as the Perfect, would continue Henry's tradition of support for seafaring enterprises.

Prester John, as envisioned in a detail from a 1561 map of the world. According to historian Daniel Boorstin, the mythical Christian king from the Indies was reputed "to combine shrewd military judgment, saintly piety, and the wealth of Croesus."

virtue and power all creatures who dwell under heaven. Seventy-two kings pay tribute to me. I am a devout Christian, and everywhere protect the Christians of our empire." This empire was apparently one of fantastic wealth, containing a river of "emeralds, sapphires, carbuncles, topazes, chrysolites, onyxes, beryls, sardonyxes, and many other precious stones." Henry hoped to enlist Prester John's aid for the war against Islam.

But more than gold, God, and glory enticed Henry the Navigator. He was equally attracted by the light that illuminates the unknown—knowledge. Although he was keenly aware that to reach Guinea or Prester John or to find a new way to obtain spices would mean added power and wealth for himself and his nation, the simple desire to know what lay beyond the dimensions of the world familiar to Europeans was equally important to him, regardless of the potential profits to be gained. Wrote Zurara: "It seemed to him that if he or some other lord did not endeavour to gain that knowledge, no mariners or merchants would ever dare to attempt it, for it is clear that none of them ever trouble themselves to sail to a place where there is not a sure and certain hope of profit."

Hoping to glean that knowledge, Henry personally questioned each captain upon his return to Sagres from a voyage down Africa's west coast, demanding detailed reports on all that he had observed. Cartographers were brought to Sagres to create comprehensive maps from the tales told by returned mariners. These reports, maps, and navigational charts were treated as a state secret and were closely guarded. Shipbuilders and scientists and artisans were brought in, all entrusted with the responsibility of devising new technology to be used for exploration. They helped perfect the use of the compass and the quadrant for navigation, but the most important tool for exploration produced at Sagres was the caravel.

On the Mediterranean, a ship's cargo-carrying capacity was its most important feature. Captains on the Mediterranean almost always sailed in familiar waters, where they knew the currents and the winds. In order to maximize profits, Mediterranean ships were large, designed to carry huge quantities of trade goods to and from their home ports; a Venetian *carrack*, for example, might weigh 600 tons or more. By contrast, Henry wanted a ship designed specifically for exploration. Trade could commence later, after Henry's mariners had discovered what there was to be found; what he needed first was a vessel that could carry explorers in unfamiliar waters, over longer distances than mariners were used to sailing, amid unfamiliar winds and currents. What his shipbuilders came up with was the caravel, which was based on the *dhow*, the small ships Arab traders used on their coastal voyages, and the *caravelas* used by river navigators in northern Portugal. Like the dhows, caravels used *lateen* (triangular) sails, which enabled them to sail more proficiently into the wind. Much smaller and more maneuverable than Mediterranean cargo vessels, most had 2 or 3 masts and averaged 70 feet in length and 25 feet across the beam. The Venetian explorer Alvise Ca'da Mosto, who sailed for Henry, called them "the best ships that sailed the seas." Caravels would carry most of the great Iberian explorers—Columbus, Ferdinand Magellan, Bartholomeu Dias, Vasco da Gama—to and from their destinations.

Despite the availability of such new technology, Henry still had to overcome two timeless obstacles—fear and ignorance. In recorded history, Europeans had gone only as far south on Africa's west coast as Cape Bojador, a point just south of the Canary Islands and about 1,000 miles north of the continent's westernmost expanse. There was nothing at Cape Bojador that marked it as special—it was not home to any fearsome peoples, treacherous reefs, tremendous waves, raging whirlpools, or particularly deadly currents. It was simply as far as Europeans had gone, and over time it had taken on the quality of a bugaboo in the minds of European mariners. Beyond Cape Bojador, it

Shipbuilding in the 15th century, from a 1486 woodcut. Caravels were so called because of the carvel construction of their hull, which meant that the planks were laid flush against one another and connected with wood pins. This method initially prevailed in the comparatively placid waters of the Mediterranean. Ships built for the rougher waters of northern Europe, such as the Baltic Sea, were characterized by lapstrake construction, in which the hull planks overlapped and were riveted together.

was said, began the infernal Torrid Zone. The notion is rooted in truth, of course—that is, in the hotter temperatures that prevail in the equatorial regions—but some Europeans believed that in the Torrid Zone the sun passed so close to the sea that its waters boiled and the land was set ablaze, a rumor given credence by the fact that off Cape Non, a few miles north of Bojador, the ocean turns red, the result of the great volume of sand deposited in the sea by winds off the desert. Others were less specific about the horrors to be found there, but there is no doubt that Cape Bojador had become a very real barrier in the collective mind of Europe's sailing men. According to Zurara, Henry's mariners believed that "this much is clear, that beyond this Cape there is no race of men nor place of inhabitants . . . and the sea [is] so shallow that a whole league from land it is only a fathom deep, while the currents are so terrible that no ship having once passed the Cape, will ever be able to return . . . these mariners of ours . . . [were] threatened not only by fear but by its shadow."

Between 1424 and 1434, Henry the Navigator dispatched 15 different expeditions to round the cape. Although the journey was not exceptionally difficult and could be made within sight of land at virtually all times, all 15 failed. At last, in 1435, an expedition commanded by Gil Eanes, who had tried and failed once before, and Afonso Gonçalves succeeded in rounding the cape and sailing some 30 to 50 leagues beyond. Although on their forays ashore beyond the cape they encountered no inhabitants, they did find the footprints of camels and humans. The bogey having been revealed as toothless, the Portuguese wasted no time in moving even farther down the coast. In 1441, Antão Gonçalves and Nuno Tristão brought Henry back a new treasure—captured African slaves. The Navigator proved interested in the captives mainly out of curiosity and out of zeal to convert them to Christianity, but the slave trade was soon thriving. The

Portuguese continued to venture even farther south, marking their progress along the coastline with wooden crosses and *padrões*: limestone pillars, seven feet tall, topped with a cross whose face bore the Portuguese royal coat of arms and an inscription stating that the king had "ordered this land to be discovered." In 1444, Dinís Dias reached Cape Verde, the westernmost point of Africa. Four years later, the traffic in slaves had grown to such a volume that Henry ordered the construction of a fort and trading post on Arguin Island, off the coast of Cape Blanco. It was the first such European outpost established overseas. Even after Henry's death in 1460, the Portuguese continued to explore along Africa's west coast, founding their lucrative forts and trading centers along the so-called Minho d'Ouro, or Gold Coast (between present-day Guinea and the mouth of the Niger River.) Sometime during this period was born the notion that if one could only succeed in rounding Africa's southernmost point, it would then be only a small matter to continue on to the Indies.

This, then, was the Portugal where Columbus found himself in 1476, an outward-looking nation pursuing new trade routes, new opportunities, new ideas, looking away from the Mediterranean. He threw himself into his brother Bartholomeo's mapmaking business, located in the Genoese quarter of Lisbon, and was soon made a partner. Mariners were eager to obtain the well-made and detailed maps prepared by the Columbus brothers; Christopher and Bartholomeo were equally eager to speak with returned ship captains and crew members and learn all that they had observed on their most recent journeys. His imagination stimulated, as always, by talk of far-off lands and peoples, Christopher especially hungered for knowledge. He yearned to know all that was known about the sea and the lands it surrounded and to that end taught himself to read and write, in Latin as well as in Portuguese.

He also returned to the sea. His work brought him contact with seafaring folk, and the amiable, curious Gen-

Caravels, from a 16th-century treatise on Portuguese exploration. The caravel's most valuable feature was its maneuverability; Portuguese sailors boasted that other ships could make the journey to the gold-laden Guinea Coast but that only a caravel could make it safely back. When rigged with square sails for fast sailing ahead of the wind, as at center, the vessels were sometimes referred to as caravelas redondas.

oan had no trouble obtaining berths aboard Portuguese vessels. By this point, Portugal had all but abandoned the Mediterranean for the Atlantic. Columbus made voyages between Lisbon, the Azores, Ireland, and Iceland. On one Icelandic voyage his ship ventured as far north as the Arctic Circle; while in Galway, in the west of Ireland, he saw in a boat two corpses that were of such extraordinary appearance that the locals asserted that they had floated there from China. (Most likely the dead people were Laplanders, not Chinese.) Back in Lisbon he read—the Bible, which was believed to be a source of secular as well as spiritual information; ancient Greek and Arabic geographers; the most enlightened modern humanists and scholars—and talked with, or to be more accurate, listened to, anyone he believed could tell him something about the sea. An idea was taking shape in his head.

He also fell in love. He met the object of his affection, Felipa Perestrello e Moniz, the daughter of a ship captain and colonial official trained by Henry the Navigator, while attending mass at the Church of All Saints in Lisbon.

This detail from a 16th-century Portuguese map shows São Jorge da Mina, the great fortress and trading center that João II ordered built on the Guinea Coast in the 1480s. Columbus made at least one voyage there while he was living with his wife, Felipa, in the Madeira islands.

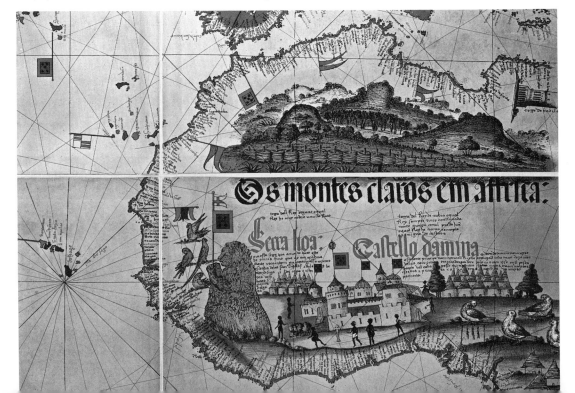

Although taciturn by nature, Columbus had a certain power to attract women. He was described by contemporaries as being taller than average, with reddish blond hair and penetrating eyes that were probably blue, although some observers described them as gray. Often silent and solemn and even melancholy, he could be friendly and outgoing, and he rarely failed to make a strong impression on others. Las Casas later wrote of him: "The Lord blessed Columbus with a special grace, which always induced others to look on him with love."

Certainly Felipa did. The two were wed, probably in 1479. The marriage represented a step up in Portuguese society for Columbus as Bartholomeo Perestrello, his deceased father-in-law, had been a member of the lesser nobility and had been rewarded for his service to Henry the Navigator—he had helped discover the Madeira island group—by being named governor of the Madeira island of Porto Santo. The title had been passed on to his son, and Columbus and his bride, accompanied by her mother, honeymooned there. While on Porto Santo, Felipa's mother made a present to Columbus of her deceased husband's maps, logs, and navigational charts, a veritable treasure trove of information on currents, wind patterns, landmarks, and ocean conditions culled from years of sailing Portugal's northern Atlantic and African routes.

The couple decided to make their home in the Madeiras and settled on Funchal, the largest island. There, Felipa gave birth to their only son, Diego, and Columbus sailed aboard Portuguese ships to the Azores and to the fortress of São Jorge da Mina (Saint George of the Mine) on the Gold Coast. His future seemed secure. Well connected through marriage, an experienced and adept seaman, he could count on receiving ever greater opportunities. In time, he might even have been asked to command a Portuguese ship on an exploring voyage along Africa's coast, a mission almost certain to bring him riches and fame, but Columbus had another route to glory in mind.

The Enterprise of the Indies

Sometime around 1483, not long after his return from Guinea, Columbus uprooted his small family and returned to Lisbon. He was possessed by an idea, one that would not let him rest. It seemed that all the monarchs of Europe wished to reach the Indies. The young king of Portugal, 28-year-old João II, was proving as single-minded in his pursuit of exploration as Henry the Navigator; his mariners had ranged 5,000 miles south along Africa's west coast, but there was still no sign of the continent's end and a passage to India. Columbus proposed a different solution. Instead of sailing south and then east, why not simply sail due west, across the Ocean Sea? One was bound to reach the Indies that way. As all educated people agreed that the earth was round, they would have to agree that it was theoretically possible to reach the East by sailing west. The crucial question thus became how long such a voyage, made out of reach of any known lands, would take.

Columbus's idea had been suggested to him by his voracious reading and had been culled from a variety of sources. As a devoutly religious man, his reading began with the Bible. In the Old Testaments's Book of Esdras, which recounts the story of the earth's creation, Columbus read: "And on the third day, Ye [God] united the waters and the earth's seventh part, and dried the other six parts." Columbus interpreted this passage to mean that the world

The "thousand battles" that Columbus endured for the sake of his Enterprise of the Indies made him bitter in later years, when he wrote that the world's "custom of mistreating me is of very old standing."

was composed of six parts land and one part water, meaning that the stretch of Ocean Sea between Europe and Asia could not be all that long. Other biblical passages also seemed to suggest as much; Columbus was particularly fond of one from the Book of Isaiah: "The isle saw it, and feared; the ends of the earth were afraid, drew near, and came." This too was deciphered by Columbus to mean that the breadth of sea surrounding the land portion of the globe could be crossed, for the ends of the earth had "drew near," that is, come closer together.

Columbus also read the work of classical and contemporary scholars as support for his theory. His chief source was *Imago Mundi* (Image of the World), a compendium of geographic thought from the classical age to the present, compiled by Cardinal Pierre d'Ailly, a learned French churchman who had been rector of the Sorbonne in the first part of the 14th century. *Imago Mundi* became Columbus's constant companion; he kept a copy always by his bedside table, even on his expeditions to the New World, and he filled its margins with notes and commentary. From it, he was thrilled to learn that "between the edge of Spain and the beginning of India the sea is short and can be crossed in a matter of days." *Imago Mundi* also provided Columbus with translated access to the thought of the foremost geographers of the ancient world. Because scientific curiosity and learning had been deemed less important than religious certainty during the Dark Ages, these ancient scholars remained some of the best sources of geographic knowledge. Other volumes that Columbus always made sure not to be without were *Historia Rerum*, by Cardinal Piccolomini, who later became Pope Pius II; *The Book of Marco Polo*, an autobiographical account of the Venetian adventurer's travels in the Orient; *Natural History* by the Roman naturalist Pliny the Elder; and *Perpetual Almanac* by the celebrated Jewish astronomer Abram Zacuto, who taught at the University of Salamanca.

From these sources and others, Columbus determined that one could reach Asia by sailing west from Europe. The chief objection to such a theory was not, as legend would have it, that the earth was flat and that one would sail right off its edge. All educated people agreed that Columbus's idea was right in theory; its drawback was putting it into practice. It was believed that the Ocean Sea was simply too wide to be crossed, that an expedition would never be able to carry the provisions necessary to complete such a voyage. The Portuguese had been able to sail so far down the coast of Africa because they did so within reach of land, putting in where necessary to replenish their supplies of food and water. But on a voyage such as Columbus proposed, there would be nowhere and no way to reprovision.

Columbus's response to such arguments was simply that they were mistaken. Pierre d'Ailly asserted that the ocean was much less wide than had been supposed, and other sources agreed. Aristotle, the great Greek philosopher who had tutored Alexander the Great, had written that the ocean could be crossed in a few days' time. Strabo, a Greek mathematician whose work Columbus had read, claimed that a few sailors had actually attempted the voyage and had returned mainly because of "a want of resolution." Columbus was certain that his own courage would never fail him. He also drew strength from the work of Paolo Toscanelli dal Pozzo, a contemporary Florentine physician, mathematician, and geographer, who in 1474 had written to Portugal's monarch Afonso V, urging him to sponsor a western expedition to the Indies. Toscanelli even included his own detailed map of his proposed western route. Although it is not certain exactly how he came to know about him—Ferdinand Columbus and Las Casas asserted that the two men corresponded, whereas others believe that Columbus somehow gained access to the Toscanelli material in the royal archives—it is clear that Columbus was thrilled to learn of a contemporary who agreed

Columbus's comments and observations fill the margins of this page of his edition of Imago Mundi. One of the jottings on the left concerns the return of the Portuguese mariner Bartholomeu Dias from his voyage around Africa's Cape of Good Hope, which spelled the end of any remaining hopes Columbus had in interesting João II in underwriting his voyage.

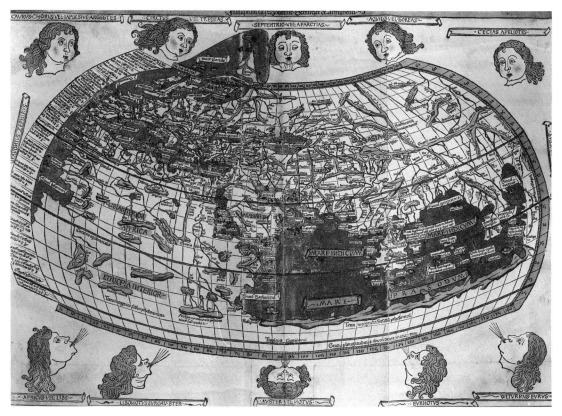

This 15th-century map was based on Ptolemy's Geography. *The father of modern cartography, Ptolemy popularized the use of longitude and latitude to divide and measure the globe and originated the now common practice of orienting a map by placing north to the top and east to the right. In Columbus's day, Ptolemy was still relied on as a geographic authority.*

with him. Las Casas wrote that Toscanelli's "map set Columbus's mind ablaze."

Columbus added sophisticated calculations, derived from his reading, to further bolster his case. As every educated person admitted that the earth was round, and as the practice of dividing a circle into 360 degrees had been in use since the time of the ancient Greeks, the earth too must be 360 degrees, Columbus theorized. The first step was to determine what portion of that 360 degrees was occupied by the known land mass—Europe, Asia, and Africa. What remained would be the space covered by the Ocean Sea, and by multiplying that number of degrees by the number of miles in a degree, Columbus would be able to arrive at the distance across the Ocean Sea in miles.

On many matters, Columbus had come to depend on

the work of Ptolemy, an Alexandrian Greek mathematician and astronomer of the 2nd century whose *Geography* was still consulted and relied on in the late 15th century. Ptolemy believed that land covered 180 degrees of the globe—exactly one-half. The rest was water. This did not suit Columbus's purposes, so on this issue he chose to disregard Ptolemy in favor of another Greek cited by Pierre d'Ailly, Marinus of Tyre. Marinus held that the earth's land area covered 225 degrees of the globe, a figure much closer to Columbus's interpretation of the Book of Esdras, which held that six-sevenths of the world's surface was land. Then, since none of these wise men—Ptolemy, Marinus, even Pierre d'Ailly—had taken into account the travels of Marco Polo, who Columbus believed had demonstrated that Asia extended much farther east than previously thought, Columbus added 28 degrees to Marinus's figure. This brought the earth's land mass to 253 degrees. Because Columbus intended to make his first landfall in the Orient at Cipango, he tacked on another 30 degrees—his estimate of how far Cipango was from Cathay. Planning to leave from the Canary Islands, which are located farther to the west than Portugal, Columbus added nine more degrees. This gave him a total of 292, meaning that according to his calculations the Ocean Sea covered only 68 degrees of the earth's surface.

His next step was to determine how many nautical miles equaled one degree. Again, Columbus had several authorities to choose from. Ptolemy figured 1 degree to be equivalent to 50 miles, but Columbus preferred the reckoning of Alfragan, a long-deceased Arab mathematician whose work he found in *Imago Mundi*. Columbus misread Alfragan and came up with a figure of 45 nautical miles in 1 degree at the equator, even less at the higher altitudes at which Columbus planned to sail. All in all, Columbus figured that the distance across the Ocean Sea between the Canary Islands and Cipango was about 2,400 nautical miles.

The only problem with Columbus's calculations was that they were spectacularly wrong. Of his sources, Ptolemy had been the closest in determining the extent of the Eurasian land mass, and even he had been far too generous. The combined length of Europe and Asia is only about 130 degrees. Ptolemy had also been closer than Alfragan and Columbus regarding the length of a degree, which is roughly equivalent to 66 nautical miles. The actual distance between the Canary Islands and Japan is more than 10,000 nautical miles.

Misguided as they were, Columbus's interpretations and reckonings offer important insights into his character. It is not as if Columbus deduced from his reading that it would be possible to reach the East by sailing west. No, the stubborn Genoan knew, as surely as he knew that his name was Columbus and that his faith was the one true faith, that there was a western route to the Indies, and his calculations proceeded from that knowledge. That is, knowing that sailing west was possible, he then looked to the wisdom of the ages for support for his argument and found, as he was certain that he would, seeming foundations for his theory. This absolute certainty, this unwillingness to admit doubt, is what defined Columbus's character. To the modern mind, it seems distinctly nonrational, even irrational, but to a man of Columbus's day, used to divining God's will directly at play in the events of the world, it would have seemed much less so. He was simply convinced that God had chosen him to find a route to the Indies and to bring the Christian gospel to the benighted heathens there. In the words of Las Casas, Columbus "developed in his heart the unshakable conviction that he would find what he said he would find, as if he had locked it away in a trunk somewhere." Still, even by the standards of his own time, Columbus's conviction set him apart. He proved to be wrong about much, but his certainty enabled him to achieve all that he did.

Determination alone would not get Columbus to the Indies, however. For that he needed a monarch willing to sponsor him. Through his marriage, Columbus was now well connected in Portugal, and in 1483 or 1484 he was able to obtain an audience with King João II, the nation's exploration-minded monarch. By this point, Columbus had added some refinements to his theory. The discovery in the previous 100 years of such Atlantic island chains as the Canaries, the Madeiras, and the Cape Verde group had given new credence to old legends about other islands said to exist to the west in the Ocean Sea—Antilia, reputed to have been settled by refugees from the Moorish wars of the 8th century, and the unnamed lands supposedly visited by St. Brendan, the Irish seafaring monk, in the 6th century. Columbus proposed now to stop off at Antilia for rest and provisions on his way to the Indies.

João would have none of it. Portugal had invested almost 50 years of effort and countless *reals* (a Portuguese monetary unit) to rounding Africa and reaching the Indies by sailing east, and João had no intention of changing course now. Moreover, the pragmatic king was less than impressed with Columbus. "The king," recorded one of the court historians, "as he observed this Christovao Colom to be a big talker and boastful . . . and full of fancy and imagination with his Isle Cypango . . . gave him small credit." Columbus said simply, "The Lord closed King João's eyes and ears, for I failed to make him understand what I was saying." Despite his skepticism, João did go so far as to refer Columbus's proposal to a committee of learned churchmen and physicians, several of whom were expert in cosmography and nautical geography. They all agreed that the venture was not feasible and counseled the monarch accordingly. In late 1484 or 1485, João officially turned Columbus down.

Shortly afterward, Columbus received another crushing blow when his wife took ill and then died. Bereft, his prospects in Portugal seemingly at an end, he took his young son, Diego, and went to Spain, Portugal's powerful neighbor on the Iberian Peninsula, where he had in-laws and friends living in the town of Palos, which served as the port for the city of Huelva, located in the region of Andalusia where the Rio Tinto and Rio Saltes meet the Atlantic. He arrived there in the spring of 1485.

Columbus made his first stop in Palos at La Rabida, a Franciscan monastery built on the outskirts of town, on a bluff high above the ocean. He hoped to persuade the monks there to take on his young son as a student; he may also have been aware that there were in residence several clergymen who were learned in science, astronomy, and geography. (Las Casas states that Columbus knew several of the Franciscans even before he arrived in Palos.) Whatever Columbus knew specifically about the men of the cloth at La Rabida, he was aware that the Franciscans had a long tradition of curiosity regarding cosmography. More than a century earlier the Scottish Franciscan John Duns Scotus had proclaimed that the earth was round and that the equatorial zones were habitable, a view that directly contradicted the traditional Christian image of the world put forth by St. Augustine, by Cosmas of Alexandria, and by Isidore, archbishop of Seville.

On his first visit, Columbus struck up a friendship with Father Antonio Marchena, an intelligent, extremely well educated cleric with a special interest in nautical studies. Marchena was fascinated by the itinerant Genoan's theories, and Columbus became a regular visitor to the monastery, where he spent long hours in debate with the monks. His intelligence and zeal regarding the conversion of the pagan souls he would encounter in the Indies also won him the support of Father Juan Pérez, the monastery's rector, who had once held a position at the royal court and was still one of Queen Isabella's personal confessors.

Pérez put Columbus in touch with the duke of Medina-Sidonia, the most powerful and richest grandee (nobleman) in all of Spain. The duke had a keen interest in the sea; he owned several shipyards, and virtually all of the Spanish caravels that Isabella had been dispatching to poach on the Portuguese territory along the Guinea coast belonged to him. He listened to Columbus with interest but for reasons of his own elected not to help him. Pérez then sent Columbus to the duke of Medina-Celi, a somewhat less magnificent grandee but one well equipped to provide the Genoan with what he asked—"three or four well-equipped caravels, and no more." Medina-Celi was even more enthused by Columbus's scheme than Medina-Sidonia had been. He was willing to underwrite the entire voyage but believed that he should first ask the permission of Queen Isabella, who had exhibited a keen interest in the Atlantic. (Ferdinand, whose home region was Aragon, was more concerned with Mediterranean affairs.) The queen responded to Medina-Celi almost immediately; he was instructed to send the interesting foreign sailor to the royal court.

Bidding his son and his clerical supporters good-bye, Columbus went to Córdoba, the nearest city where the

Columbus and his son Diego with the monks at La Rabida, the Franciscan monastery at Palos, as painted by the great 19th-century French artist Eugène Delacroix.

Los Reyes.

Los Reyes Católicos receive the sacraments. At their first meeting, there was an intuitive understanding between Columbus and the gentle, spiritual Isabella, but Ferdinand was much less impressed by the would-be explorer from Genoa.

royal court was in the habit of calling. (At the time, Spain had no fixed capital where the court maintained a permanent residence. Instead, it followed the monarchs as they moved from city to city, overseeing the country's affairs.) Ferdinand and Isabella were elsewhere when Columbus arrived, but he found ways to occupy his time. He obtained an audience with Pedro González de Mendoza, cardinal of Spain and bishop of Toledo, an immensely powerful and wealthy churchman sometimes referred to as Spain's third king. Mendoza listened respectfully to Columbus's proposal but tried to temper his enthusiasm by explaining that most of the kingdom's money was being devoted to the ongoing war with the Moors. Columbus was unimpressed. How, he wanted to know, could Mendoza quibble about money when Columbus was offering Spain all the treasures of the East? The interview concluded unsatisfactorily as far as both men were concerned.

There were better days. Minstrels sang the praises of Córdoba's "fragrant blossoms, sturdy mules, and pretty women," and Columbus again fell in love, this time with Beatriz Enriquez de Harana, the cousin of a friend he made there. They had one child together, Ferdinand, who would become his father's biographer and travel with him on his last voyage. Although Columbus and Beatriz never married and apparently had a falling-out at some point— she did not attend his funeral—he always took pains to see that she was well provided for.

At last the court came to Córdoba and Columbus was granted his royal audience. He met the monarchs in the Alcázar, the splendid palace and fortress built by the Moors centuries earlier, when Córdoba was one of Europe's leading cities, known as the Athens of the West for its riches and the achievements of its famed scholars. Now, Columbus was trying to convince Ferdinand and Isabella, whose marriage 16 years earlier had united Spain's largest and most powerful kingdoms, that he was the man to lead

Spain into a new age. Somewhat bluff and impatient, happier with activities such as falconry, jousting, and wenching than court business, Ferdinand paid only cursory attention to what the quietly eloquent Columbus had to say, but Isabella—who was close to Columbus in age, similar in temperament, and like him had reddish hair and blue eyes—was moved, almost against her better judgment, particularly once Columbus began to speak of the souls to be won for Christianity. No decision was given, but Columbus had reached Isabella. She ordered him placed on the royal payroll and referred the matter to a committee of priests and scholars headed by Hernando de Talavera, a bishop and another of the queen's confessors.

There followed what Columbus later characterized as "the years of great anguish," spent following the Talavera commission to Salamanca and other cities, answering its members' endless questions, trying to refute their arguments. Columbus's effectiveness as his own advocate was mixed. His enthusiasm and certainty were almost enough to carry all before him, but he could be curiously unpersuasive, almost tongue-tied, in rebutting objections, of which the Talavera commission had many. The members argued, quite correctly, based on their own learning and investigation, that Asia was much farther away than Columbus had supposed. No ship, they argued, could sail that distance; no ship could carry enough provisions for a voyage of that duration. They asked why, if it was indeed possible to sail west to the Indies, God had not chosen to reveal it to his faithful until this moment and why he had chosen as the instrument of his supposed revelation an obscure Genoan, who to this point had not proved himself to be outstanding in any way. To most of these questions Columbus offered no response; according to Las Casas, "he always remained silent on the most important of these matters."

There were good reasons for his silence. Columbus's knowledge was of a kind more akin to faith; he was more certain that he could reach the Indies than he was adept at explaining why. Many of the men of the commission were also individuals of great faith, but their belief had led them to different conclusions; as the history of religious conflict over the ages demonstrates, when two differing faiths collide, the result is often an impasse or destruction, not conversion or a meeting of the minds. Although Columbus's belief in himself and his idea was boundless, he was intimidated by the intellectual achievements and abilities of his interrogators and realized that he could not match his learning against theirs; instead, he retreated to his stubborn insistences. Finally, much of the reasoning his questioners used against him was based on religious doctrine. With the Spanish Inquisition (a religious tribunal founded by Ferdinand and Isabella in 1478 to root out Jews and Moors who had converted to Christianity insincerely) condemning to death as heretics hundreds of individuals annually, Columbus was prudently careful how he responded to such sophisticated examination.

The Spanish Inquisition was established by Ferdinand and Isabella in 1478 to impose Catholic orthodoxy on all of Spain. Until it was abolished in 1834, the Inquisition was greatly feared for its use of torture and the death penalty to root out heresy. This scene of one of its tribunals in session was painted by Francisco Goya in the early 19th century.

Among the most devout of men, he certainly did not intend his Enterprise of the Indies as a challenge to the Christian view of the world. On the contrary, he believed that it would result in the greater glory of his god.

This still left the commission with little to go on. They gave Columbus repeated opportunities to explain himself but were left instead only with his unyielding insistence that he knew he could do it. The deliberations took years; Columbus grew weary and discouraged. He became something of a joke at court and was mocked as a madman, the fool who thought he could sail the Ocean Sea. Impatient, in 1488 he asked for and received King João's permission to return to Lisbon. The unfortunate Columbus arrived just in time to witness the return of the fleet of Bartholomeu Dias, which had at last succeeded in rounding Africa's southernmost point, named by João the Cape of Good Hope. Although Dias's terrified crew forced him to turn back to Portugal without reaching India, his feat meant that Portugal had discovered the eastern route to the Indies. Recognizing that João would now have less interest than before in a western passage to the Orient, Columbus returned to Spain without even speaking with the king. Before doing so he prevailed upon his brother Bartholomeo, with whom he had been briefly reunited in Lisbon, to go to France and gauge the interest of that country's monarch in funding westward exploration.

There were further blows to be endured. In the last weeks of 1490, the Talavera commission delivered its report. Calling Columbus's theories "mad" and his conclusions the product of "colossal" errors, the report stated that the members of the commission could "find no justification for their Highnesses supporting a project that rests on extremely weak foundations and appears impossible to translate into reality to any person with any knowledge, however modest, of these questions." They had all but called Columbus insane. With the rejection, Columbus's stipend was cut off. He sunk into poverty, his hair turned white, and legend has it that he was forced to burn his father-in-law's charts and maps in order to heat his shabby rooms.

Apparently defeated, Columbus returned to Palos and La Rabida in the autumn of 1491. He had not renounced his dream, but it did appear that it would never be realized in Spain. As they had once before in a dark period of his life, the Franciscans lifted Columbus's spirits. Father Juan Pérez, who had maintained his connections at court, pointed out that the Talavera report was just a recommendation, that Ferdinand and Isabella had the final word, and that they had yet to deliver a final verdict. Moreover, he added, it was said that Isabella was favorably disposed toward Columbus, and with the war against the Moors going well, she might be willing to reconsider his proposal. Pérez even went so far as to write to Isabella and then to go to the royal court at Seville, where he pleaded Columbus's case to the queen's advisers and the monarchs themselves.

Pérez's brief had the desired effect. Late in the year, a royal messenger presented Columbus with a letter bearing Isabella's seal. It was accompanied by a purse filled with a rather considerable sum of money to be used "so that he could dress himself decently, buy a horse, and present himself to her Highness."

Columbus caught up with the court around Christmastime at Santa Fe, a small village near Granada that was serving as the royal command post for the final assault against the Moorish stronghold. This time, however, Columbus had come not to plead but to demand. No longer was he willing to settle for three or four well-equipped caravels. Hardened and somewhat embittered by the years of scorn and waiting, sensing the outlook was favorable, he told los Reyes Católicos that he was willing to undertake the Enterprise of the Indies for a price: He must be raised to the nobility; awarded the hereditary titles of admiral of the Ocean Sea and viceroy and governor of all lands that he should discover; given a 10 percent commission on all trade between the new lands and Spain, including commerce in jewels, precious metals, and spices; and allowed to invest up to one-eighth of the total cost in any ship doing business with his discoveries.

Rarely had anyone, let alone a foreigner, dared to display such cheek at the Spanish court. Unused to being dictated to, the monarchs summarily refused Columbus's terms and sent him on his way. With his mule and Juan Pérez, Columbus set off for Seville, planning to head for France, where he hoped Bartholomeo had met with some success.

Back at court, the debate continued. Columbus's assessment of the situation had not been too far off; the monarchs and their advisers had agreed, before the arrogant Genoan's demands had angered them so, that the venture was worth sponsoring. Luis de Santangel, a shrewd businessman who was also Ferdinand's treasurer, was especially interested in the scheme, seeing in it an opportunity for massive profits through trade with the East. He persuaded the monarchs to reconsider, pointing out that until Columbus actually achieved something, their risk was virtually nothing—just the cost of outfitting a fleet of three small caravels. But should he succeed, Santangel reasoned, the power, glory, and riches to be gained by Spain would be beyond imagining. In that case, Columbus's 10 percent would seem a small share, and he would certainly have earned his noble titles. Even more convincing was Santangel's willingness to underwrite the greater share of the expedition himself.

A horse and rider were sent after Columbus, and he was brought back to court. After several months of further haggling, a contract between the monarchs and their new captain-general was signed. Known as the Capitulations, it awarded Columbus all that he had asked for. At last, it seemed that the Enterprise of the Indies was to become a reality.

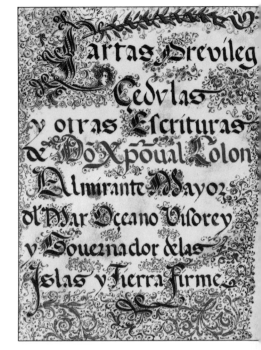

The frontispiece for the Capitulations, as the agreement between Columbus and the Spanish monarchs regarding the Enterprise of the Indies was called.

To the Indies

On May 23, 1492, a local official read from a wrought-iron pulpit a solemn proclamation, marked with the official seal of Ferdinand and Isabella, to the silent congregation at the Church of St. George, a brown-and-yellow limestone structure in the town of Palos. Rumors about the decree had been bandied about for days, and the crowd that had gathered for mass that Sunday filled the entire church and spilled out-of-doors, filling the portal known as *la puerta del embarcadero*, the door to the pier, which gave onto a red clay path that ran from the church to the quays on the Rio Tinto. The assembly, Columbus and Father Juan Pérez among them, heard the town notary inform the citizens of Palos that as punishment for past smuggling transgressions, they were ordered to give to the Crown, as represented by one Christopher Columbus, "at your burden and cost," two caravels, equipped for a journey of a year's duration and manned with a crew given four month's advance pay. The ships were to be ready within 10 days.

The Enterprise of the Indies was to cost Ferdinand and Isabella even less than they had imagined, for they—or one of their advisers—had hit upon the idea of simply impounding two of the vessels they needed. Further indication that the monarchs still regarded the venture as dubious was also given from the pulpit that day. Anticipating that finding enough able hands willing to ship out under a foreigner of limited nautical experience for a voyage into the unknown would be difficult, the monarchs

Columbus's clerical supporters from La Rabida bid him farewell as the small fleet prepares to leave Palos for the Indies.

had the notary announce that all criminal and civil charges pending would be dropped for anyone willing to sign on for the voyage.

The announcement pleased virtually no one. Columbus was delighted to be receiving his ships at last, of course, but he could not have relished the idea of commanding a crew of jailbirds on a journey that would require an exceptional degree of courage and discipline on the part of each of its members. The townspeople were appalled at the monarchs' arbitrary decree, and the good friars of La Rabida who had backed the project also did not approve of its depending on the uncertain virtues of three shiploads of convicts for its successful completion.

Fortunately, Columbus had made some friends in Palos. Aside from the clergy, his most important ally—although their relationship was always an uneasy one—was Martín Alonso Pinzón, head of a seafaring family and regarded as the best sailor in Andalusia. Pinzón owned several of his own ships and had made many voyages to Guinea, the Canary Islands, and elsewhere. Always hungry for money and glory, Pinzón supported Columbus because he saw that the Enterprise of the Indies offered the opportunity for both, although he was jealous that the Genoan was likely to claim the greater share and therefore

Among the essential documents provided Columbus by Ferdinand and Isabella was a letter of introduction to the Grand Khan, seen here in an illustration from a 1524 edition of The Book of the Wonders of the World, *by Sir John Mandeville, a pseudonymous 14th-century chronicler whose accounts of his alleged travels imbued Europeans with many whimsical ideas about Africa and the East.*

never quite fully accepted Columbus's authority. Still, Pinzón wanted the venture to succeed, and as something of a local hero he had no problem recruiting the area's sailors for the journey. Frequenting the taverns and inns haunted by the region's mariners while ashore, he enticed them with tales of the fabulous adventures that awaited them, of the gold-roofed palaces and jewel-bedecked women of the Orient, of the fame that would be theirs. Said Yanez de Montilla, a Palos sailor who heard Pinzón's pleadings: "Martín Alonzo put much zeal into enlisting and encouraging crewmen, as though the discovery was to be for his and for his children's sakes."

With the support of Pinzón, Columbus had little problem putting together his crew. It numbered 90 in all, including himself; of that number, only 4 were convicts, and they were sailors whom Pinzón had worked with and trusted. The crew was entirely Spanish, except for Columbus, three other Italians—a fellow Genoan, a Calabrian, and a Venetian—and one Portuguese. Each ordinary seaman received the equivalent of about seven dollars in gold per month as wages. There were three surgeons, a marshal—Diego de Harana, cousin of Beatriz's, Columbus's mistress—who acted as a sort of police officer for the fleet, and an interpreter, Luis de Torres, a converted Jew who knew Arabic, which supposedly would help him converse with the Grand Khan—as Europeans referred to China's ruler—and other Asian potentates. Columbus himself had been given letters of introduction to the Grand Khan by Ferdinand and Isabella.

Palos provided Columbus with the smaller two ships of his fleet, caravels called the *Niña* and the *Pinta*. The *Niña* was so called after its owner, Juan Niño, who with his brother Pedro Alonso headed a shipping family second in prominence in the region only to the Pinzones. A fast and agile ship, the *Niña* had a cargo capacity of about 60 tons and was not longer than 70 feet in length. It was initially equipped with three lateen sails, although Columbus had

Martín Alonso Pinzón (left), Columbus's early supporter and sometime nemesis. In Palos, the elder Pinzón was given the lion's share of the credit for the success of the Enterprise of the Indies. His younger brother Vicente Yáñez, who captained the Niña, *remained loyal to Columbus and later achieved renown as an explorer by discovering the mouth of the Amazon River and the great Mayan civilization on the Yucatán Peninsula.*

the mainmast and the foremast rigged with square sails in the Canary Islands. Vicente Yáñez Pinzón, brother of Martín Alonso, served as the *Niña*'s captain; its owner shipped out as its master, the officer second-in-command, who maintained direct responsibility for the crew, sails, and rigging. The slightly larger, square-sailed *Pinta* was commanded by Martín Alonso Pinzón; its master was another Pinzón brother, Francisco.

The flagship was renamed by Columbus the *Santa María*. It belonged to Juan de la Cosa, a well-known mariner and shipowner from the region of Galicia, in northwest Spain; for that reason it was known originally as *La Gallega* (the Galician). The Crown, through Columbus, arranged with de la Cosa to rent his vessel, which was larger than the others and of the type the Spanish and Portuguese called a nao rather than a caravel. It had a deeper hull and higher bulwarks than the others and could carry about 100 tons. De la Cosa sailed with his ship as owner and master; Columbus acted as its captain and the captain-general for the entire fleet.

It took far longer than 10 days to prepare the ships, but by August 2 everything was in order. The night before, each member of the crew went to confession and attended mass at the Church of St. George. The following morning, shortly before dawn, the fleet set sail, moving slowly down the Rio Saltes, past La Rabida high above them on the bluff and finally out to sea, the banner of the expedition and Ferdinand and Isabella's royal ensign fluttering from the mainmast and the mizzenmast.

The immediate destination was the Canary Islands, where additional supplies were to be taken on. On previous voyages, Columbus had noticed that easterly winds prevailed at that latitude. He believed as well that the islands were on the same line of latitude as Cipango, so he intended to take advantage of the favorable winds and make due west from the Canaries. The fleet reached Grand Canary Island in six days, but its stay there was prolonged when it was learned that the rudder of the *Pinta* had broken off its hinges. While awaiting the necessary repairs, Columbus spent many days ashore at the castle of Beatriz de Bobadilla, the charming, young widowed governor of the island of Gomera, whose acquaintance he had made at court and with whom he was reputed to be amorously involved. But once the *Pinta* was ready, Columbus did not tarry. By the time the full moon rose on September 6, the tiny fleet was more than 100 miles from Gomera, sailing west on the Ocean Sea.

It seemed to the always mystically inclined Columbus that heaven was smiling upon his great venture. Each day dawned gloriously—"What a delight was the savor of the mornings," the captain-general wrote in his log—and the sea air was "like April in Andulusia; the only thing wanting was to hear the song of the nightingale." Backed by the easterly trade winds, the ships made excellent time, sometimes covering almost 200 miles in a single day. "We are

This 16th-century sandglass was probably similar to the ones Columbus used aboard his ship. Called an ampolleta by Spanish mariners, it measured a half hour and was used to mark the watches. After every eight turns of the ampolleta—approximately four hours—the watch was changed. In later years, a bell was rung each time the ampolleta was turned, giving rise to the expression "eight bells" for the change of shift.

sailing as though between a river's banks," Columbus reported in his log, and he exulted in the routines of shipboard life—the changing of the watch after eight turns of the *ampolleta*, an hourglass containing a half hour's worth of sand that was the only device for measuring time available on ships of the day; the ship's boys offering a hymn to the morning each day at dawn; the communal intoning of the Our Father, Hail Mary, and Apostle's Creed each day at sunset, followed by the singing of Salve Regina.

The captain-general was as sure of his course as he was of his faith—"West; nothing to the north, nothing to the south." Direction was measured with a compass that was mounted in a binnacle on deck. Just barely competent with the instruments available for celestial navigation—the astrolabe and the quadrant—Columbus relied on the method known as dead reckoning to chart his ships' position, meaning that he depended on a combination of his experience, his intuition, and guesswork to figure where his fleet was at any given moment. Speed was commonly measured by letting out behind a ship a line that had been tied into knots at regular intervals and to which a small wooden float, called a *corredera*, had been affixed at its end. A sailor then counted how many knots were let out in a fixed number of ampolletas; hence the use of the term *knots* to measure a ship's rate of speed. By multiplying the average rate of his ship's speed by a fixed amount of time, a captain could arrive at a rough estimate of the distance he had traveled in that period. Columbus did not even make use of the corredera, preferring instead to trust instinct and his power of observation. In most instances he measured speed by sight, basing his estimate on the amount of time it took waves to move from the prow to the stern or on how long it took bubbles left from the wake of the ship to disappear from view.

Columbus's seafaring instincts were nothing less than extraordinary and have been commented on by virtually everyone who has written about him. According to a

French biographer, Jean Charcot, "Columbus possessed a *sense of the sea*, that mysterious intelligence which in the glory days of sailing enabled captains lacking proper scientific knowledge to find, as it were by a sense of smell, their course in the boundless expanse of the Seven Seas." The American historian Samuel Eliot Morison carefully reconstructed and retraced Columbus's epic first voyage, using modern scientific and navigational equipment, and determined that Columbus's estimate of his rate of speed was only off by five percent. Ironically, the distance figures that Columbus recorded in the "false log" that he kept for the consumption of his crew "so that his men would not get frightened or discouraged if the voyage became too long" were almost invariably dead accurate. Columbus was less likely to have been bothered by the possibility of a miscalculation of distance than were the sailors under his command. They were sailing into the unknown; he was quite sure of where he was going. Having made his "westing"—that is, set his fleet on a course along the line of latitude at which Cipango was believed to lie—Columbus had only to maintain that course in order to reach his

This late-15th-century engraving portrays Columbus as a lone mariner sailing fearlessly onward under the banner of Christ and the dove of peace to confront the allegorical terrors of the deep and add to the Spanish crown "the regions of almost another world that he discovered."

destination. His estimates of speed and distance would simply tell him when; if he miscalculated, it would mean only that the ships would arrive sooner or later than he had expected.

The optimism of the crew was shorter lived than that of their commander. Shipboard routine grew old quickly for enlisted men. Captains slept in bunks in cabins in the forecastle—Columbus kept near his bed a seaman's trunk that contained, among other items, a Bible and *Imago Mundi*—but crew members slept on the deck, wherever they could find a suitable spot. Only one hot meal was served each day, at the changing of the 11 o'clock watch, and the variety of the meals was necessarily limited—salted meat, cheese, barreled sardines, anchovies, hardtack, sometimes lentil, chick-pea, or bean soup. When not working, sailors sometimes fished from the ship's deck; fresh fish for lunch was regarded as a delicacy.

It was not long before, in Las Casas's words, the crew "began to grumble about the voyage and about the man who had got them into this fix." All educated people of the day knew that the world was round, but the men of the crew were something other than scholars; it was likely that no one besides the officers could read and write. One cannot be certain that they feared that the ships would sail off the edge of the earth, but they were no doubt familiar with a wide range of the legends and stories—tales of sea monsters and boiling seas and endless whirlpools—that seafaring men told about the unknown places on the globe. Such fears of the unknown should not be dismissed lightly, for they were perhaps the greatest obstacle that Columbus had to overcome. It had taken the brave captains of Portugal years to conquer their fear of what lay beyond Cape Bojador, and the objections of those who had opposed the Enterprise of the Indies were rooted, at least in part, in an unwillingness or inability to confront the unknown, which in the minds of certain members of the Talavera commission had become the unknowable as well. If God had meant for man to sail the Ocean Sea, he would have revealed it long before now, went such arguments. For the men of Columbus's crew, the concerns were more elemental—fear for their safety and for their life.

The grumbling began in mid-September, when the fleet drifted into the Sargasso Sea, that expanse of still water in the Atlantic covered with floating, brightly colored algae—brown, yellow, and green—that resembles grass or a vast meadow of seaweed. Columbus described it as "great banks of very green grass that looks as though it was just recently cut from the earth." At first the men were overjoyed, believing that the sargassum heralded the presence of a nearby island, but after days passed with no sign of land, they grew morose. Few mariners had ever before reported this phenomenon, and the sailors feared that the ships would become entangled in the thick sargassum and held fast. With his customary assurance, Columbus pronounced that "grass does not hamper navigation," and the fleet sailed on, although at a slower speed, for the trade winds had weakened, and on some days opposing winds prevailed. Although the change in the wind hindered the fleet's progress, it was not unwelcome, even to the captain-general. The crew had come to believe that the prevailing easterlies were a bad omen, even though they hurried the ships to their destination, for they wondered how they would be able to sail home against such winds. Columbus knew that at higher latitudes in the Atlantic, westerly winds prevailed, and he intended to use those to power his fleet on its return voyage, but he welcomed the shift in breezes nonetheless for the small boost it gave to his crew's flagging faith. "This head wind was utterly indispensable to me," he wrote in his log, "because my sailors by now must have been quite worked up against me, thinking that there were no winds capable of bringing me back to Spain."

Columbus consistently proved himself less adept at judging the hearts of other men than he did at fixing a navigational course, but on this matter he was correct. His men were quite worked up against him, and subsequent events did nothing to improve their mood. The fleet plowed through the sargassum, only to face a new menace—colossal waves, 100 feet high by 100 feet wide, the remnants of tropical storms that had rocked the area. The ships performed nobly, climbing the towering swells, holding their own in the troughs, and in his journal Columbus indicated that he regarded their successful passage as a wonder akin to the parting of the Red Sea, one more sign that his mission was divinely favored: "A miracle of this sort has not come to pass since the Egyptians took to pursuing Moses and the Jews he had freed from slavery."

But the men of the crew were awaiting a different kind of miracle—the appearance of land on the horizon. Despite the presence of several varieties of seabirds—pelicans, herons, petrels, albatross, sea swallows, frigate birds, and wheatears—by October land had still not been sighted. "The people could stand it no longer," Las Casas wrote of the crew, "and complained of the long voyage." Some members plotted mutiny together. Columbus was alternately encouraging—he "cheered them as best as he could, holding out good hope of the advantages they would have" in the Indies, according to Las Casas—and stubborn, informing them that he was dead set on reaching the Orient and that nothing they could say would cause him to alter his course. On October 7, after repeated sightings of flocks of birds flying to the southwest, Columbus accepted Martín Pinzón's advice and altered the fleet's course in that direction. The ships and sailors had now covered about 2,400 miles, more than the distance Columbus had calculated as separating Cipango and the Canaries. The change of course left the crew unsatisfied, and they continued to plead with the captain-general to turn the ships around. Columbus refused to acquiesce, replying to all objections, according to a seaman present, by saying: "If we do not find land you are permitted to cut off my head; that way you can sail home in peace." Martín Pinzón

(continued on page 81)

Widening the Globe

Although it took several years for the full implications of what Columbus had discovered to become manifest, it became apparent soon after his first voyage that the world was a much different place than educated Europeans had assumed. One need only compare the maps drawn by Florentine scholar Paolo Toscanelli dal Pozzo (above) and mariner Juan de la Cosa (pages 76–77) in order to see colorfully and clearly delineated the change that had taken place in the European view of the world. For Toscanelli, the Renaissance physician whose scholarship Columbus cited in convincing Ferdinand and Isabella to sponsor him, the globe was occupied by one land mass, comprising Europe, Africa, and Asia. His conception of the Mediterranean world is detailed and accurate, but more remote regions bear little resemblance to what is known today of their geography. By contrast, the world as charted several decades later by de la Cosa, who sailed with Columbus and then commanded several voyages of his own, is much more recognizable to the modern viewer. To Europeans, it was as if Columbus had added an entire new world to the globe.

Most scholars believe that this portrait of Columbus, by an anonymous 16th-century Italian artist, most closely resembles his actual appearance.

Genoa, the "noble and powerful city by the sea" where Columbus was born. Over generations, Columbus's ancestors had migrated to Genoa from the mountains to the northeast. When Columbus was born in 1451, his family probably lived in the Portoria district, just inside the city's outer walls.

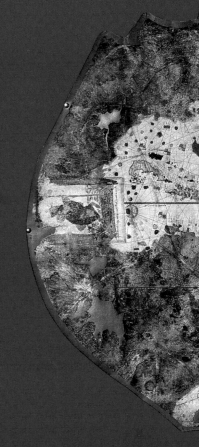

A protective Mary, styled by the artist of this 1505 painting as the Virgin of the Good Winds, spreads a cloak over a kneeling Columbus (first figure to her left), his ships' officers, and some natives of the New World. Columbus's flagship, the Santa Maria, *probably closely resembled the ship at center foreground.*

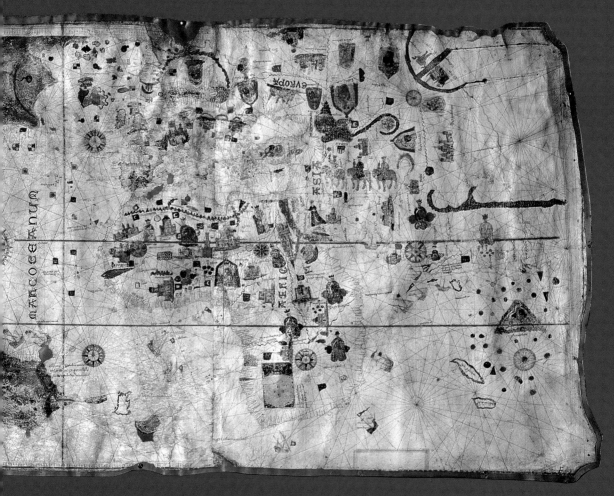

Juan de la Cosa's map, most likely drawn around 1500. De la Cosa sailed with Columbus on his first two voyages and later made four expeditions to South America; this map is generally regarded to be the first of its kind of the New World.

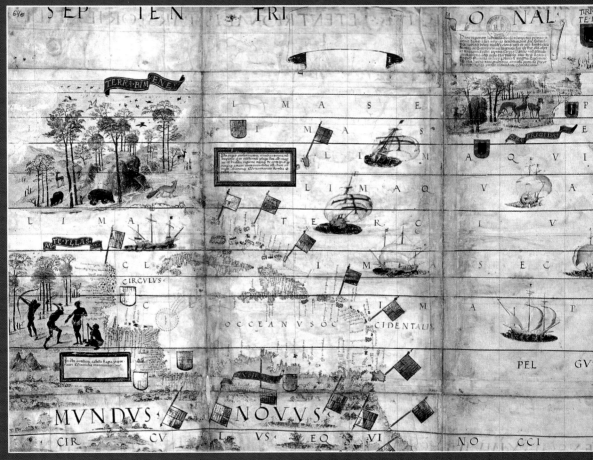

The inhabitants of the New World; a detail from the larger map seen on these pages. Both Spain and Portugal used the Indians of North and South America as slaves in order to extract the two continents' immense wealth in precious metals.

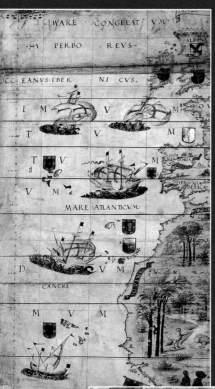

A Portuguese map of the New World from the early 16th century. Notice that the mapmaker had some knowledge of the topography, flora, and fauna of North America—the cartographer has included mountain ranges, hardwood trees, deer, bears, and a fox. He was apparently more familiar with the native inhabitants of South America, where Portugal's only possessions in the New World were located.

The island dominions claimed for Spain by Columbus; a detail from the larger map on these pages. It was not until after Columbus's death that Spain began to appreciate the full significance of his discoveries, which gave it the beginnings of a vast colonial empire in the New World.

The coat of arms earned at such high cost by Columbus. In the lower lefthand quarter of the shield is a representation of the myriad islands he discovered; in the lower righthand quarter are anchors representing his noble title of admiral of the Ocean Sea.

(continued from page 72)

remained enthusiastic, crying at the fainthearted, "¡Adelante! ¡Adelante! [Onward! Onward!] We've just barely left and you're thinking of turning back?"

Around October 8 or 9, a final meeting of the captains was convened aboard the *Santa María*; Columbus agreed to set sail back to Spain if land was not sighted within three or four days. On the night of October 11, the captain-general spotted the eerie flickering glow on the horizon that he thought resembled the light from a "little wax candle rising or falling." Hallucination? Optical illusion? Moonlight playing off the distant waves? No one has ever determined for sure, but most historians and biographers agree that the ships were still too far away from land for Columbus to have spied the light from a hut or a torch. Several hours later, the lookout on the *Pinta* shrieked that he had spotted land. At midday on October 12 the Spaniards and their Genoan commander went ashore on the island they called San Salvador and greeted the inhabitants of the New World. Convinced that he had reached the Indies, Columbus named them "Indios," or Indians. (For similar reasons, the islands Columbus discovered are often referred to collectively as the West Indies.)

San Salvador was disappointing, but Columbus was not discouraged, for he was certain that something marvelous—a gold mine or the palace of the Grand Khan—must be nearby. The fleet sailed off in search of Cipango or the land where gold was born or China—any of them would do. Following the directions of the captive Indians, Columbus set a zigzag course, first southwest, then west, southeast, east, southwest, and south. This path took them to a number of small islands—named by Columbus Santa María de la Concepción, Fernandina, and Isabela; there were others as well—similar to San Salvador. Their inhabitants were naked, friendly, and poor; they slept in hammocks—"beds similar to cotton nets, and made like suspenders"—and subsisted on cassava bread, an unleavened food, made from manioc roots, that the Europeans

Bartolomé de Las Casas, the Dominican bishop and historian whose General and Natural History of the Indies *made use of Columbus's log, which has since disappeared. Las Casas went to Hispaniola in 1502 as a planter; about a decade later he became the first priest ordained in the New World. He eventually became known as the Apostle of the Indies for his impassioned efforts to obtain fair treatment for the Indians.*

The staple food of the Indians Columbus encountered on his first voyage was cassava bread, which the Indians baked from the roots of an indigenous plant. The Europeans found it neither toothsome nor nourishing.

found unpalatable; they all assured Columbus, as did his guides from San Salvador, that he would find gold on the next island he came to. Columbus remained undismayed. Marco Polo, Toscanelli, Ptolemy, and virtually all of the cosmographers whose work he had relied on had testified to the existence of a large number of islands off China and north of Cipango; all these small outcroppings seemed to the captain-general confirmation that he was nearing his destination. While keeping an eye out for gold, Columbus pronounced his satisfaction with the islands' other attractions: "I never grow tired of looking at this splendid vegetation, so different from our own. I believe that it contains many plants and shrubs that would be highly valued in Spain as sources of dye, medicine, and spices." Not having found the wealth in precious metals that he sought, Columbus convinced himself that the islands abounded in spices.

Meanwhile, his guides persisted in discussing a large island to the southwest that they called Colba. It is known today as Cuba, but Columbus believed that the Indians must have been referring to Cipango. The three vessels reached Cuba on October 28, landing somewhere on the island's northern shore, probably in today's province of Oriente. Ashore, the disappointed adventurers found only some deserted crude huts and "a dog that did not bark." Columbus was now willing to admit error: Colba was not an island but part of a continent, most likely a region of China that Marco Polo called Mangi. The fleet moved eastward, exploring the island's northern shore, investigating every bay and river mouth, entreating the local Indians with hawks' bells, glass beads, and shiny mirrors. Along the way, the fleet lost Pinzón and the *Pinta*, for Martín Alonso decided, on his own, to investigate a report about an island to the north, known to the Indians as Babeque, whose inhabitants were said to gather on the beach at night to hammer gold into bars by candlelight. Columbus was furious at Pinzón's disappearance, but he did not go to look for him. The natives kept on referring to "Cubanacan," meaning a city on the island of Cuba, but to Columbus the word sounded like Great Khan and could only mean that his palace was near. Understanding at last that the Indians were referring to a "great city" with a "great king," Columbus dispatched Luis de Torres (the interpreter trained in Hebrew and Arabic) and several others inland to investigate. They found that the great city consisted of about 500 huts; although the "men from the sky," as the Indians regarded the Europeans, were treated well, they were disappointed not to find any evidence of gold, and they found the village to be somewhat shabby. Torres, armed with Ferdinand and Isabella's letter of introduction to the Khan, found it hard to believe that no one understood Arabic. They did report back to Columbus about an interesting local custom, however; Columbus noted in his log that his emissaries encountered "many people who were going to their villages, with a firebrand in the hand, and herbs to drink the smoke thereof." This is the first mention in European literature of the practice of smoking tobacco.

But the leaf was not gold, and seeing no practical application for this discovery, Columbus decided to take his two ships east, across the strait known as the Windward Passage, where the Indians had let it be known there was another great island. At nightfall on December 5 the *Santa María* and the *Niña* dropped their anchors in a natural harbor Columbus named San Nicolás Mole, on the west coast of an island he called la Isla Española (the Spanish Isle) for its "grandeur and beauty" and "its resemblance to the land of Spain," according to Las Casas. Hispaniola, as the island is more commonly referred to, was not Cipango, but it overwhelmed Columbus nonetheless. "It is a desirable land," he reported to Ferdinand and Isabella, "and once seen is never to be relinquished." The Europeans spent the next couple of weeks beating along Hispaniola's northern coast, recording the island's natural beauty, observing its exotic flora and fauna, and trading on a small scale with the Indians, who here seemed to have ample access to the precious metal Columbus and his men coveted and were willing to exchange large amounts of it for the trinkets the Spaniards offered. Closer observation of Hispaniola did not lessen its appeal to Columbus, whose wonder and enthusiasm are evident in the letter he later composed for his royal patrons:

> In it there are many harbors on the coast of the sea,
> incomparable to others which I know in Christendom, and
> numerous rivers, good and large, which is marvelous. Its
> lands are lofty and in it there are many sierras and very
> high mountains. . . . All are most beautiful, of a thousand
> shapes, and all accessible and filled with trees of a
> thousand kinds and tall, and they seem to touch the sky;
> and I am told that they never lose their foliage, which I

can believe, for I saw them as green and beautiful as they are in Spain in May, and some of them were flowering, some with fruit, and some in another condition, according to their quality. And there were singing the nightingale and other little birds of a thousand kinds in the month of November, there where I went. There are palm trees of six or eight kinds, which are a wonder to behold on account of their beautiful variety, and so are the other trees and fruits and herbs; therein are marvelous pine groves, and extensive champaign country; and there is honey, and there are many kinds of birds and a great variety of fruits. Upcountry there are many mines of metals, and the population is innumerable. *La Spañola* is marvelous, the sierras and the mountains and the plains and the champaigns and the lands are so beautiful for planting and sowing, and for livestock of every sort, and for building towns and cities. The harbors of the sea here are such as you could not believe in without seeing them, and so the rivers, many and great, and good streams, the most of which bear gold. . . . There are many spices and great mines of gold and of other metals.

This anthropomorphic gold figure was made by a South American Indian tribe in the period before European contact. The New World did boast incredible material and cultural riches in the form of precious metals and complex civilizations, but Columbus was repeatedly frustrated in his attempts to locate them.

Despite the paradisiacal qualities of Hispaniola that he so evocatively delineated, Columbus was most interested in the gold, as he knew his king and queen would be. They had sent him to the Indies to find riches, not a land suitable for settlement and farming, no matter how desirable it might be. It is likely that even Isabella, for whose sake Columbus commented on the Indians' suitability for conversion to Christianity, would have regarded his mission as a failure if all he had returned with was news of a beautiful island and nothing to fill the royal coffers. After all, solid evidence—aside from his own unshakable certainty—that Columbus had actually reached the Indies was conspicuously lacking.

But there was gold on Hispaniola. On December 16, Columbus invited a local chieftain to dine with him aboard the *Santa María*. Columbus was much impressed by the potentate's dignified and solemn bearing, even more so by his solid-gold jewelry. The ships continued along the coast, anchoring at night near the shore so that the natives could come out and speak and trade with them. On the night of December 22, more than 1,500 Indians visited the ships. Columbus continued to be impressed by their friendly ways. They were "very cowardly," he wrote in his log, "fit to be ordered about and made to work, to sow and do aught else that may be needed." At another point, he observed:

> To rule here, one need only get settled and assert authority over the natives, who will carry out whatever they are ordered to do. I, with my crew—barely a handful of men—could conquer all these islands with no resistance whatsoever. The Indians always run away; they have no arms, nor the warring spirit. They are naked and defenseless, hence ready to be given orders and put to work.

This woodcut of Columbus trading with the Indians accompanied a 1493 edition of the Santangel Letter, as his report to Ferdinand and Isabella was known. He was delighted by the willingness of the Indians to trade gold and food for cheap trinkets.

On December 24, Christmas Eve, the *Santa María*, with the *Niña* just ahead of it, was all but becalmed not far offshore a bit east of Cape Haitien. The two ships had spent the last two days hugging the shore as they slowly advanced toward the region of Hispaniola known as the Cibao. Columbus was eager to get there and was driving his crew hard; the Cibao was ruled by a powerful and apparently wealthy chieftain known as Guacanagari, who had sent the strange visitor in the giant ship a stunning belt with a buckle in the form of a mask with "ear, tongue and nose made of pure gold." The difficulty of the maneuvers they had been required to perform while negotiating the treacherous shoreline waters had kept Columbus and his crew awake for 48 hours; at last, after the turning of the 11 o'clock ampolleta, the exhausted captain-general retired to his cabin. It was a calm night; the feast of the Nativity was but an hour off, and almost all of the fatigued crew settled down to grab a little sleep before dawn announced the celebration of the birth of Christ. Somehow, a ship's boy was left with the rudder "for a moment" while the helmsman snatched a nap. Gently, almost imperceptibly, the *Santa María* ran aground on a coral reef.

Alerted by the scream of the ship's boy, Columbus was on deck in an instant, but it was too late. The jagged coral had torn several holes in the hull, and the *Santa María* was beyond saving. Guacanagari's subjects helped the Europeans transfer provisions and supplies to the *Pinta*, impressing Columbus—who recorded in amazement that "not even so much as a piece of string was missing"— once again with their virtues. The captain-general was even moved to observe that the heathen Indians practiced Christianity's golden rule: "They love their neighbors as themselves."

The catastrophe meant the end of the expedition, for Columbus could not take a chance on anything happening to his one remaining ship, the *Niña*. As always, Columbus saw the divine at work in this latest episode and interpreted the sinking as God's way of telling him that he was to found a colony on the spot, near the gold mines of Guacanagari's people. Enthused by the prospect of carving out huge properties and growing rich from gold, 39 Spaniards, led by Diego de Harana, volunteered to remain behind. A fortress was constructed out of timbers from the wreck of the *Santa María* and equipped with the ship's guns. A moat was dug around it; a year's supply of wine, bread, and grain was stored in the fort's underground cellars. Columbus confided to his journal his certainty that the tiny colony would prosper: "When I return here from Castile I shall find such riches extracted from this land that the king and queen, within three years' time, will be able to prepare and carry out the reconquest of the Holy Sepulcher in Jerusalem." (This was a reference to the much-discussed new crusade to free the Holy Land from the Muslim infidel.) On January 2, a farewell party was held—Guacanagari was an honored guest—and two days later the *Niña* set sail for Spain.

A New World

In some ways, the return voyage was as terrifying as the journey out had been. The adventurers had survived the unknown only to be threatened with destruction before they could tell of the wonders that they had seen. As Columbus had foreseen, easterly winds prevailed at the higher latitudes in the Atlantic, and the caravels again made exceptional time. (A couple of days out from Hispaniola, the *Niña* and the *Pinta* had been reunited. Pinzón apologized for his willfulness, explaining that he had gotten lost after separating from the fleet. Glad to have the company and another ship available in case of mishap, Columbus forgave him.) But rough weather also prevailed in the winter months, and in mid-February the two ships sailed into the teeth of a titanic storm. Columbus's log described the tempest: "The sea began to swell and the sky grew stormy"; the ocean rose "in fierce rebellion, such that we could neither advance nor make our way out of the waves attacking the caravels and breaking against them." Icy rain and winds lashed the frightened sailors; the angry sea rolled over the decks, and "if the caravels had not been very good ships, and well repaired, they would surely have been lost." In the turbulence, the *Niña* and the *Pinta* were separated once again. The storm raged for three days. Terrified that his ship might go to the bottom and deny him an opportunity to tell of his great discovery, Columbus hastily prepared a summary of his log, sealed it in a cask, and tossed it overboard, hopeful as ever that Providence would look after his interests. The

A romantic portrayal of the lavish reception accorded Columbus by Ferdinand and Isabella at Barcelona upon his triumphant return from the New World.

petrified crew vowed to make a pilgrimage to the nearest shrine, clad only in their shirts as penance, if the Blessed Virgin would deliver them from the threatening ocean.

The weather eased enough for the beleaguered *Niña* to put in at Santa Maria, the southernmost of the Azores Islands, where the crew made their pilgrimage and were threatened with arrest by the island's Portuguese authorities, who refused to believe Columbus's story and insisted that the Spanish vessel must have been "trespassing" in Portuguese waters off Africa's west coast. Blustering and threats by Columbus gained his men's release, but at sea the gale blew up again with renewed ferocity. The wind tore the sails from the *Niña*'s masts, driving the small craft headlong toward the Portuguese coast. At daybreak on March 4, a desperate Columbus recognized the mountains just north of the mouth of the Tagus River. With little real choice, he elected to put in at Lisbon for repairs, trusting on the benevolence of João II, Spain's enemy and the monarch whose service he had left.

Fortunately, the sometimes ruthless João was feeling magnanimous. He instructed Lisbon's harbormaster to provide Columbus with what he needed, then summoned the discoverer for an audience at the monastery where he was staying in order to escape the epidemic that was ravaging Lisbon. Columbus took great satisfaction in informing the king—one of many who had doubted him—of all that he had discovered. He presented as evidence the Indians who had been seized. João's courtiers were stunned at the insolence of the foreign "braggart" and begged their monarch to kill him. Instead, João cursed himself, lamenting aloud, "Why did I let slip such a wonderful chance?"

The repaired *Niña* reached Palos on March 15, 1493, followed shortly afterward by the *Pinta*. Pinzón had reached port in northern Spain about two weeks earlier and sent word to Ferdinand and Isabella that he wished to come to court, but the monarchs denied him the op-

The Santa María, *as depicted in a woodcut from a 1493 illustrated edition of the Santangel Letter. After Columbus's flagship was wrecked on a reef, its timbers were used to construct the fortress at Navidad.*

portunity to steal Columbus's thunder, instructing him to
wait for the arrival of the captain-general. The disconsolate
Pinzón then sailed for Palos, where he went directly to
his home and died within the month.

Columbus stepped ashore as Spain's grandest hero. A
copy of his letter had already been dispatched overland
from Lisbon to the royal court, and news of his discovery
was spreading. (Columbus's letter to Ferdinand and Isabella is often referred to as the Santangel Letter because
although intended for the enlightenment of Ferdinand and
Isabella, it was directly addressed to Luis de Santangel,
the treasurer who was one of Columbus's strongest backers.
Court protocol forbade addressing the monarchs directly.)
In early April, Columbus received the reply he had been
awaiting—a letter addressed to him as "Admiral of the
Ocean Sea, Viceroy and Governor of the islands that he
hath discovered in the Indies." These were exactly the
titles that had been promised him in the Capitulations.
The monarchs instructed him to begin immediate prepa-
rations for a second voyage and summoned him to court
at Barcelona. The final entry Columbus made in his log
reflects his sense of triumph over all who had doubted
him:

> Of this voyage I reflect that the will of God hath
> miraculously been set forth . . . by the many signal
> miracles that He hath shown on the voyage and for
> myself, who for so great a time was in the court of Your
> Highnesses, with the opposition and against the opinion of
> so many high personages of your household, who were all
> against me, alleging this undertaking to be folly.

Columbus's journey to court was a triumphal procession.
Peasants and grandees turned out to see the exotic cav-
alcade of bold adventurers, Indians in plumed headdresses
and fishbone-and-gold ornaments, and brightly colored
parrots and other birds. Hired servants followed Columbus
and his officers, carrying items of pure gold and amber.
In the courtyard of the royal palace in Barcelona, the

nobility rose as one when Columbus entered, an honor usually reserved for the land's most important grandees. In the palace's great hall, where Columbus knelt at the feet of Ferdinand and Isabella, the monarchs made him rise and sit at the queen's right hand while he described his adventure. At dinner with the monarchs that evening, Columbus was served "covered"—with a cover over his plate, placed there after the king had tasted his food. This high honor, called *salva*, was usually reserved for persons of royal blood.

The monarchs had good reason for their gratitude, for if Columbus had done what he said he had—and at this point no one doubted that he had reached the Indies—he had virtually made Spain Portugal's equal on the sea by providing it with its own route to the Orient. His discovery sparked a diplomatic dispute between the two nations, each of which wished to secure exclusive control over their own trade routes. Unable to reach agreement between themselves, they submitted their argument to the papacy, whose jurisdiction over lands not previously under the rule of a Christian monarch was accepted by all of Europe. The new pope, Alexander VI, was a Spaniard who owed his election, in part, to the support of los Reyes Católicos, but his ruling was the essence of compromise. At his behest, Spain and Portugal agreed to draw an imaginary line down the Atlantic almost 400 leagues west of the Azores. All undiscovered lands to the west of the line established by the Treaty of Tordesillas, as their agreement was called, would belong to Spain; everything to the east to Portugal.

By the time this agreement was reached Columbus was back at sea on his return voyage to Hispaniola, at the head of a convoy of 17 ships carrying 1,200 men. His mission was to establish a trading post and permanent colony on the island. This time there had been no problem filling out the crew, all of whom were volunteers eager to make their fortune on Hispaniola. In addition to sailors, the ships carried *hidalgos* (members of the lesser nobility);

farmers; a cavalry troop to conquer the Indians, six priests to convert them, and several fierce mastiffs to keep them terrified; and a supply of horses, pigs, sheep, and grain.

Once again the weather was fine, and the ships made good time. Day after day, in the words of the fleet's physician, Diego Alvarez Chanca, "the sun rose on a sea as smooth as polished marble." Columbus ordered a slightly different course than on the first voyage, wishing to explore the many islands the Indians had told him lay to the east of Hispaniola. As before, his navigational sense was uncanny—he had, instinctually, chosen both the best way to go to and return from the New World—and in early November 1493 the fleet made its first landfall, on an island Columbus named Dominica. It was one of the group known today as the Leeward Islands; as the fleet made its way north and then west, it encountered dozens more, too many to explore—scores of the Virgin Islands and Puerto Rico, which caught the eye of a passenger named Juan Ponce de León. On an island Columbus named Santa Cruz (Holy Cross), a small exploratory party was attacked by several Indians, members of a fierce tribe of man-eaters called Caribs by the more peaceful inhabitants of the other islands. (The term is the base for the word *cannibal*.) One Spaniard was killed; a couple of the Indians were captured, and "once on board they struggled like Libyan lions in chains," according to Pietro Martire d'Anghiera. "There wasn't a single man who could stand the sight of them, so horrific, menacing and cruel an appearance had nature given them."

The encounter served notice on the Europeans that the New World and its inhabitants were not quite as idyllic as had been supposed. Further confirmation was not long in coming. On November 23, a small party was put ashore on Hispaniola, some 25 miles east of Navidad, in order to explore the area as a possible site of settlement. They discovered two corpses, bound to a tree, badly decomposed, but with long beards, like Europeans. Columbus

(continued on page 96)

On Columbus's second voyage, he discovered scores of islands in the Caribbean; he would ultimately claim to have found and named more than 700 in all. This illustration is from an edition of the Santangel Letter published in the Swiss city of Basel in the 1490s.

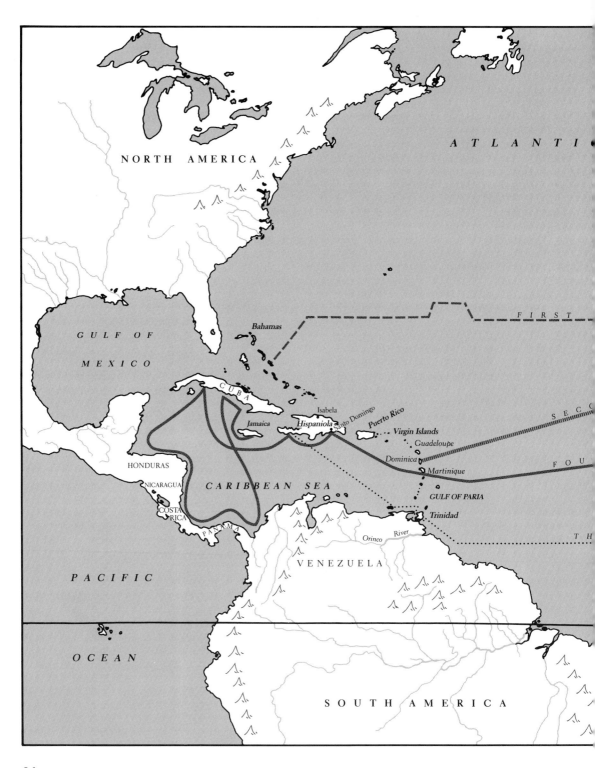

ATLANTI

NORTH AMERICA

GULF OF

MEXICO

Bahamas

FIRST

CUBA

Isabela

Jamaica

Santo Domingo

Puerto Rico

SECO

Hispaniola

Virgin Islands

Guadeloupe

Dominica

FOU

CARIBBEAN SEA

Martinique

HONDURAS

GULF OF PARIA

NICARAGUA

COSTA
RICA

Trinidad

PANAMA

TH

Orinco   River

PACIFIC

VENEZUELA

OCEAN

SOUTH   AMERICA

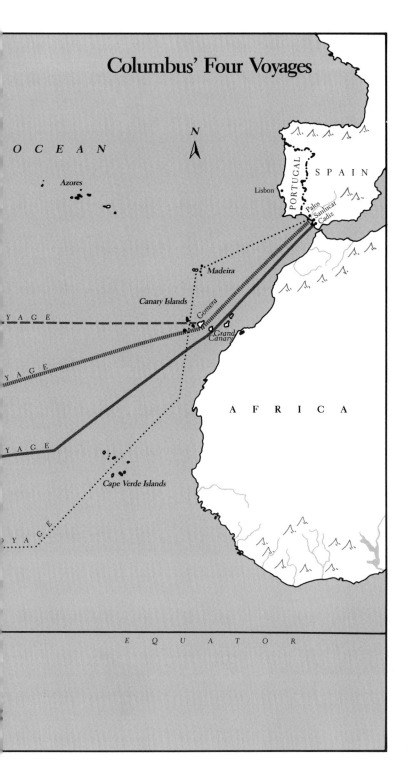

Columbus' Four Voyages

O C E A N

N

Azores

PORTUGAL

SPAIN

Lisbon

Palos
Sanlúcar
Cadiz

Madeira

Canary Islands

Gomera

Grand
Canary

Y A G E

Y A G E

A F R I C A

Y A G E

Cape Verde Islands

O Y A G E

E Q U A T O R

The routes of Columbus's four epic voyages to the New World.

(continued from page 93)

hurried his fleet to Navidad. It arrived at nightfall on the 27th. Signal torches were sent, and the ship's guns were fired, but there was no response from shore. In the morning, the grisly truth was discovered. Navidad was a charred ruin; the corpses of its defenders were discovered for miles around. There were no survivors.

Columbus soon pieced together the grim truth. Discipline among the Spaniards who had remained behind had quickly broken down. They desired gold and women, and the Indians had both. Raiding parties plundered the countryside. Understandably, the Indians soon tired of this behavior; a chieftain named Caonabo organized several highly effective ambushes and then set upon Navidad with a huge war party. The 10 defenders of the fortress who

The first page of the first Spanish edition of the Santangel Letter, which according to Columbus was written "in the caravel off the Canary Islands, on the fifteenth of February, year 1493." He added a postscript on March 4, while awaiting repairs on the damaged Niña in Lisbon.

had survived the forays into the interior were easily over-run.

The grim discovery cast a pall over the enterprise. Columbus had no easy explanation for this catastrophe; he ordered the fleet to sail east in search of a site for a new settlement. Bucking strong head winds, the ships took 25 days to sail 32 miles, stopping at last on January 2, 1494, at a peninsula that offered shelter from the fierce breeze. Here, Columbus decided, the new colony would be built; he named it Isabela, after his royal sponsor.

It was an angry group of Spaniards that set to founding Spain's first trading post in the New World. The massacre had weakened their confidence in Columbus's leadership abilities, and some openly mocked him for having characterized the natives as gentle and peaceful folk. Most had shipped out to make what they thought would be an easy fortune, and they resented being ordered to clear land, dig canals, and build huts, especially when the order came from a Genoan, not a Spaniard. Moreover, it soon became obvious that the site of Isabela had been poorly chosen, for it offered no easy access to fresh water and was infested with mosquitoes. Columbus's governing style—he was alternately distracted, given to long silences and hesitation before he spoke, then intense; keen on enforcing discipline, then lax—did not help matters.

Determined to make sure that he and the Crown received their allotted share of Hispaniola's gold, Columbus was initially firm about allowing parties to investigate the interior, but after only 4 days at Isabela, as an attempt to raise morale, he sent out an armed band of 20 or so Spaniards under the command of Alonso de Ojeda, of whom Las Casas wrote: "He was very devoted to the Virgin Mary, but was always the first one to spill blood whenever there was any dispute or conflict." This made him a good man for the job; he returned after two weeks bearing gold nuggets and word of a lush valley where gold could be found in the streams. This raised spirits at Isabela, but not too

The ill-fated fort at Navidad, built from the wreck of the Santa María *and armed with its guns, was probably a cruder structure than this woodcut from a version of the Santangel Letter indicates.*

much. About 300 of the men were sick, either from malaria or the unfamiliar food and water. Provisions were being expended rapidly, and no progress had been made toward clearing fields and planting crops.

Although disappointed at the gold yield and aware that Ferdinand and Isabella would be doubly so, Columbus had no choice but to send 12 of his ships back to Spain with a letter asking Ferdinand and Isabella for more supplies—footwear, food, firearms, wine (a dietary staple for the Spanish), pack animals, and medicine. Although he acknowledged that there were many ill at Isabela, Columbus assured the monarchs that all was going well. The only reason the ships were not filled with gold, he explained, was that the colony lacked beasts of burden, so the Spanish had no way to transport the precious metal.

With unrest continuing at Isabela, Columbus decided to explore the interior himself. With much fanfare, he set off south from Isabela on March 12 at the head of a force of several hundred men. One of those, Michele de Cuneo, succinctly summarized the tenor of the journey: "On that trip, we spent 29 days with terrible weather, bad food, and worse drink; nevertheless, out of covetousness for that gold, we remained strong and lusty." The gold mine that Columbus expected to find remained undiscovered; leaving 50 men in the interior with instructions to build a fort, he returned to Isabela to find things unchanged. Discontent was rife, and Columbus's decision to throw several of the more troublesome dissidents in irons did nothing to ease the tension. A firm hand was in desperate need at Isabela, but Columbus opted to distance himself from the situation. First he dispatched Ojeda and 400 men to San Tomás, the fort in the interior, with instructions to relieve the small garrison there; most chose instead to rampage about and terrorize the Indians, extorting gold from them and carrying off their women and children as mistresses and slaves. While this was going on, Columbus set sail for Cuba, still convinced that Cipango or the Grand Khan was not far off. He left his brother Diego in charge at Isabela.

In command of three caravels, he spent about eight weeks exploring what he called "the world of the Indies," which was in reality Cuba's southern coast and Jamaica. In mid-June, with the ships the worse for wear because of some severe weather, he was forced to return to Isabela. Still convinced that Cuba was a province of China, he forced all the men of his crew to sign a deposition attesting to their certainty that the island was part of the "continent of the Indies." Soon afterward, Columbus collapsed, sinking into what Las Casas called "a pestilential sleep that robbed him of all his faculties and strength." Modern interpreters believe that Columbus was suffering from either a severe attack of gout or arthritis or a nervous breakdown brought on by stress and exhaustion. There is no doubt that his body was wracked by either arthritis or gout for the rest of his life, and at times he would wander in and out of lucidity. Columbus later said that on this journey he had gone "33 days without tasting sleep" and that this deprivation left him temporarily blind. In any event, he had to be carried ashore when his ships reached Isabela at the end of September.

Indians attempt to repel a Spanish landing in the New World. Although they greatly outnumbered the European newcomers, Hispaniola's Indians were unable to unite against them, and they were overawed by the horses, dogs, and weapons of the Spanish.

His recovery was swift, but he was unable to bring order to the rapidly deteriorating situation in the colony. Because the colonists refused to farm, the settlement was still dependent on provisions from Spain, and disease and hunger were epidemic. In Columbus's absence, his brother had attempted to restrain the Spaniards running loose in the interior. The fort's commander, Pedro Margarit, grew infuriated at being asked to explain his behavior and with the help of a malcontent priest, Father Buil, commandeered three caravels and sailed back to Spain, where they spread tales at court of Columbus's heavy-handed rule. On Hispaniola, a state of virtual warfare now existed between the whites and the Indians, particularly in the interior, where the Spaniards' predations had not lessened.

Unable to rein in his own men, Columbus decided to terrorize the Indians into quiescence. In the early spring of 1495 he led an expedition of conquest into the interior. At least one major pitched battle was fought, but the Indians, who greatly outnumbered the Spanish, were frightened by the latter's weapons—crossbows and harquebuses—

Even more devastating to the Indians of Hispaniola (and later on elsewhere in the New World) were the diseases the Spanish introduced, for which the Indians had no immunity. Smallpox, a virus that causes high fevers and severe skin eruptions, was among the most deadly. By the middle of the 16th century, mistreatment and disease had killed all of the island's estimated 250,000 Indians.

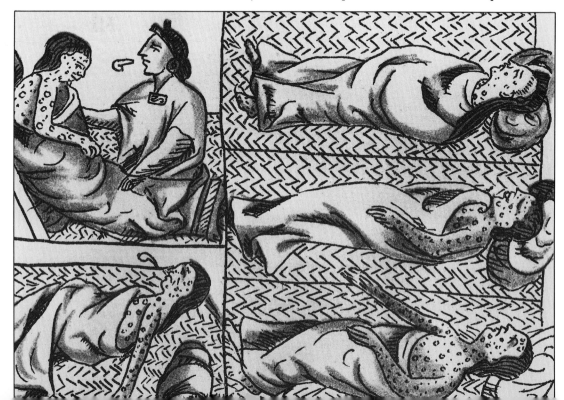

the horses they rode, and the huge mastiffs they unleashed upon their adversaries. The natives fled into the mountains, from where they carried on scattered resistance, but by the end of the year they had been effectively subdued. Hundreds were killed; hundreds more were made slaves. According to Ferdinand Columbus, the result was that "a Spaniard could venture alone wherever he pleased, enjoy the products of the soil and the local women free of charge, and have natives carry him on his shoulder for as far as he should desire." Five hundred Indians were shipped as slaves to a disapproving Ferdinand and Isabella, who advised Columbus that they wished the natives to be converted, not enslaved. Columbus also instituted a system whereby each Indian male over the age of 14 was required, on pain of death, to produce enough gold every 3 months to fill a small flask. Disease and continued mistreatment finished the work Columbus began; by the middle of the 16th century, Hispaniola's Indian population had been reduced from an estimated 250,000 to nothing.

With the Indians at last thoroughly subjugated, Columbus finally heeded his royal patrons' repeated injunctions to return to Spain. The stories told by Margarit and Buil made the monarchs nervous, as had indications that Hispaniola was not quite as rich as Columbus said it was, and they had some questions they wished to ask him. He left the island on the reliable *Niña*, with one other caravel, on March 10, 1496. Both ships were dangerously overloaded, as 225 Spaniards, desperate to return home, crowded aboard. (Normally, the ships would have carried about 50 men.) Individual rations on the return journey were limited to six ounces of cassava bread and a cup of water each day. At several points the famished Spaniards proposed eating the Indians Columbus was transporting, but he managed to prevent this. At Cádiz, where Columbus's second voyage ended in June 1496, onlookers were stunned to see that the disembarking Spaniards were skeletal, with drawn and anxious faces "the color of saffron."

rante de nauios para las Indias.

Defaming and Disparagement

Disillusionment had set in. Another procession was organized, but it was less festive and triumphant than the first, and when Columbus reached Valladolid, the city in west-central Spain where the court was temporarily in residence, he found Ferdinand and Isabella less effusive in their praises and gratitude than previously. The reports from Hispaniola had disturbed them, and they were beginning to wonder if, despite his undeniable skills as a mariner, Columbus was the best man to govern the colony. The monarchs well knew how willful and difficult Columbus could be, and they cited as an example of his arrogance his naming his brother Bartholomeo *adelantado*, or provincial governor, of Hispaniola, a title that only they had the power to confer. The enterprise that had seemed so promising just four years earlier was now rife with questions. Although they were not sure exactly what Columbus had found, Ferdinand and Isabella were beginning to realize that it was not the Indies. The promised gold had not materialized in the volume expected, and Isabella would not accept Columbus's proposal that the Crown profit from the sale of the slaves he sent back. (The more pragmatic Ferdinand was less shocked by the suggestion, but he too ultimately agreed that Spain should convert, not enslave, the inhabitants of the New World.) Columbus read to the monarchs a list of the 700 islands

A wizardly Columbus, from a 1621 treatise on navigation. In his later years, as his spiritual bent grew more pronounced, Columbus did take on an otherworldly air—he claimed to navigate by heavenly guidance, and some of his crew on the last voyage took to calling him the Divine for his uncanny skills— but to his opponents on Hispaniola, he was the devil incarnate.

he had discovered, but they wished to know of what practical value these islands would be to Spain if they were as barren of spices and metals as Hispaniola was proving itself to be. Always a good barometer of the monarchs' opinions, the courtiers began to mock Columbus, sometimes addressing him sarcastically as the "Admiral of the Mosquitoes," a place said to be the "ruin and the grave of Castilian gentleman."

Columbus's demeanor did not help; worn from his trials, he acted hesitant and unsure of himself, lapsing into long silences. To Isabella, he seemed "not the same man." He attributed the disfavor into which he had fallen as an indication that God was unhappy with him for the pride he had displayed after the success of the first voyage, and as penance he donned the plain brown robe of a Franciscan, girdled with "the knotted cord of devotion." This penitential garb would be his daily costume for the rest of his life, and while in Spain he often boarded at monasteries and religious dwellings. With his white hair and beard, now often unkempt, he looked more than ever the mystical ascetic.

Columbus could have lived out the remainder of his days in comfort on the rich pension the Crown was willing to grant him, but as Salvador de Madariaga, one of his biographers, put it, he "felt in the strongest of fashions that the Indies were his property," and he was unwilling to relinquish personal control over Hispaniola. Although Ferdinand and Isabella were growing wary of their Genoan subject, they did have a project for which they felt he would be suited. Spies at the Portuguese court reported that King Manuel, called the Fortunate, who had succeeded João II and inherited his exploratory projects, believed in the existence of a great southern continent opposite Africa in the Ocean Sea and was preparing to mount an expedition to search for it. Determined to protect its investment in Hispaniola, the Spanish crown did not wish its Iberian rival to gain a foothold in the region.

Columbus was more than eager to undertake the quest for the southern continent, particularly as he believed that one was more likely to find gold in southern climates, as Aristotle and many ancient scholars had advised. Once done with his exploratory work, he would call at Hispaniola and deliver the 300 colonists Ferdinand and Isabella wished him to recruit.

It took all of 1497 and the first months of 1498 to ready the ships and men. No one was clamoring anymore to go to Hispaniola, so Ferdinand and Isabella ordered the jails to be emptied, and it was from convicts that the recruits were chosen. Thirty women also sailed for Hispaniola; the first European women in the New World had to pledge their labor in exchange for passage and promise to marry soon after arrival.

A detail from a 1500 map drawn by Juan de la Cosa, who sailed with Columbus on the first two voyages, shows Hispaniola and Cuba as well as part of South America.

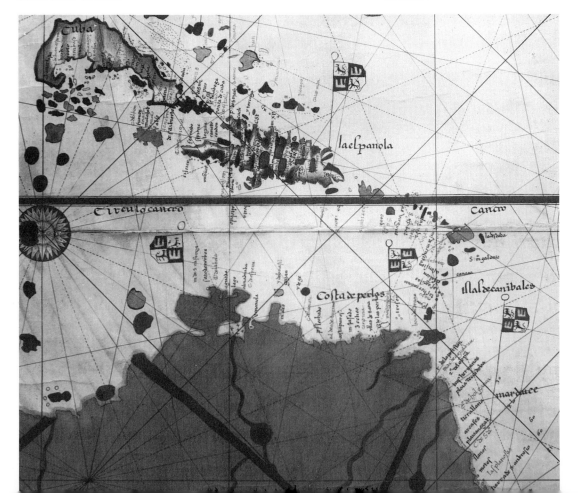

This engraving, probably executed in the 16th century, shows Columbus's fleet among the Indian pearl divers of Margarita Island. In actuality, Columbus simply sighted and named the island; it was his former shipmates, Alonso de Ojeda and Juan de la Cosa, who profited from Margarita's pearls.

Six ships departed Sanlúcar de Barrameda, the port at the mouth of the Guadalquivir River, in the last week of May 1498. Three of those, carrying most of the colonizers, sailed directly for Hispaniola. The remaining three, under Columbus's command, set forth on the *rumbo austral*, the southern voyage, so called because it would take them below the equator. Columbus put credence in Aristotle's dictum that similar elements were to be found at similar latitudes the world over, so he planned to first sail south, to the waters off the Guinea coast, where he would make his westing until reaching the unknown southern continent. There, he trusted, he would find gold, which he once described as "a thing most excellent, for he who possesses it may have what he will in this world."

The outward passage was relatively uneventful, although the ships were becalmed for nine days in the broiling equatorial doldrums southwest of the Cape Verde Islands, at the approximate latitude of Sierra Leone. Much of the provisions spoiled and some of the crew feared that they would be roasted alive, but fresh trade winds soon arrived to spirit the fleet along. On July 31, it reached the southwest corner of a large island, where the skyline was dominated by three mountains. Columbus accordingly named the island Trinidad (Trinity) and spent the next three days exploring along its southern shore. Twice, his men went ashore; once, a group of Indians came near, but when the Europeans attempted to entice them into trade, they let fly a hail of arrows and vanished into the forest. While anchored at Trinidad's southwestern tip, the ships were menaced by a huge tidal wave, which lifted them high into the air and then seemingly flung them at the bottom of the sea. Relatively little damage was sustained, but Columbus decided that it would be prudent to move on. Before doing so he named the waterway, which is, in fact, a narrow strait separating Trinidad from the mainland of Venezuela, Boca del Sierpe—Mouth of the Serpent.

On Columbus's orders, the fleet headed due north, making for some mountains that dotted the horizon. They were sailing across the Gulf of Paria; ahead of them was the Paria Peninsula, which juts to the east almost to Trinidad. On August 5, Columbus and some of his men came ashore near the tip of the peninsula. This marked the first time that Europeans had set foot on the South American mainland, although Columbus did not regard the moment as unduly significant, believing that he had found yet another island. Several days were spent sailing to the west—the wrong direction—in search of an outlet to the sea. One of the caravels was sent to reconnoiter ahead; its crew reported upon their return discovering four river channels—the mouth of what is today known as the Rio Grande. On the 13th, Columbus found the outlet he was looking for and sailed through its turbulent waters, where the fresh water of the bay met the salt water of the ocean, into the Caribbean Sea. In a hurry to reach Hispaniola, Columbus did not stop to explore an island to the west

Pietro Martire d'Anghiera drew this map of Hispaniola, probably around the year 1500. A Florentine humanist who spent much time at the Spanish court, Martire is often referred to by the Anglicized version of his name, Peter Martyr. His letters did much to spread the news of Columbus's discoveries throughout Europe.

Columbus's detractors blamed him for unleashing a legacy of colonial oppression in the New World, which is one reason why his historical reputation suffered for so long after his death. This drawing was done by Maya Indians in Mexico to illustrate their suffering under their Spanish overlords.

that he called Margarita; had he done so, he would have discovered the pearls that made very wealthy men of the Spanish traders who followed him, Alonso de Ojeda among them.

It was only once out at sea that Columbus came to his own understanding of what he had found. He confided to his log that he believed he had discovered *un otro mundo*, another world, "a very great continent, until today unknown." Nor was that all, for he now believed that this discovery was the most wondrous of all—the gateway to the Garden of Eden. His justification for this belief was his characteristic blend of reason, faith, certainty, and imagination. Learned Europeans had long believed that the Garden of Eden, or Earthly Paradise, was a real place situated on the globe but unreachable to man. The Book of Genesis, from the Old Testament, stated that the "Lord God planted his garden eastward in Eden," a passage interpreted by Columbus and many of the authorities of *Imago Mundi* to mean at the farthest eastern reaches of the Orient, which is where Columbus believed he was. He offered further evidence: The force of the current that emerged from the 4-mouthed river in the Gulf of Paria sent fresh water 20 miles out to sea. Could this not be the great river that Scripture said flowed from the Tree of Life in the Garden and gave rise to the four great rivers of the world—as Columbus listed them—the Ganges, the Tigris, the Euphrates, and the Nile? For Columbus, there was no doubt, although he was unable to explain how this was geographically possible: "I believe that all this water might indeed come from there, though the place be far away."

The Admiral of the Ocean Sea sailed from paradise straight into hell. He had reason to hope that conditions on Hispaniola had improved, for he had left Bartholomeo with instructions to move the settlement from Isabela to a more hospitable location. Santo Domingo, located at the mouth of a large river on the opposite (south) side of the island from Isabela, was better suited to be the site of a permanent settlement, but the problems the Columbus brothers had in governing had not lessened. In his older brother's absence, Bartholomeo had been bedeviled by an outright rebellion led by Francisco Roldán, whom Columbus had appointed the colony's chief justice. Roldán and 70 followers had taken to the wild, where they had made common cause with the Indians. Few at Santo Domingo rejoiced at the viceroy's return, and Columbus never felt that he had enough men he could count on to put down the mutiny. Instead, he negotiated, eventually restoring Roldán's title and granting him and his followers land, gold, slaves, and free passage home when they wanted it. The land grants contained the foundation of the notorious *repartimiento* system that the Spanish eventually used to settle much of their holdings in the New World; a settler was given a designated plot of land and all the Indians who lived on it as his personal slaves.

Columbus's attempt at appeasement earned him little goodwill at Santo Domingo. Resentment at being governed by "foreigners" continued unabated, fueled by the Columbus brothers' practice of using their control over provisions to enforce compliance with their dictates. Rebellion became commonplace; the Columbuses, said the dissidents, "were always quick to torture, hang, and behead." Suffering terribly from his various afflictions, including the return of his eye trouble, Columbus seemed to some to have come unhinged. Certainly, this was Isabella's judgment upon receiving his rambling letter reporting his belief that he had found the Garden of Eden and expressing other far-fetched geographic theories. The alarming reports she had been hearing, Columbus assured his queen, could be attributed to jealousy and the fact that virtually everyone on Hispaniola was a vagabond. The epistle also contained a virtual confession of failure—Columbus pleaded with the monarchs to send him a wise and impartial administrator of justice and even volunteered to pay the official himself.

All this was too much for Ferdinand and Isabella. Deciding, in Ferdinand's words, that Columbus was "a good admiral but not a good viceroy," they dispatched one of their most trusted officers, Francisco de Bobadilla, to right the situation on Hispaniola. Bobadilla was granted almost absolute power to carry out his mission. He arrived at Santo Domingo on August 23, 1500, and was treated almost immediately to the sight of a couple of corpses swinging from the gallows; they were, in Las Casas's words, "still fresh, having been hung just a few days before." Questioning Diego Columbus, who had been left in charge while his brothers hunted rebels in the interior, a horrified Bobadilla learned that five more rebels were to be hanged the next day. The ringleader of the most recent uprising had escaped this fate; Columbus had ordered him flung into the sea from the top of a watchtower.

This was all that Bobadilla needed to hear. He clapped Diego into irons and seized all his possessions, ensuring himself of the support of the already overjoyed populace by declaring that henceforth everyone would be free to gather as much gold as they liked. Upon their return to Santo Domingo, Bartholomeo and Christopher Columbus suffered the same fate, and then all three were sent back to Spain for trial. It was a bitter downfall for the proud Admiral of the Ocean Sea, who had much time to contemplate his outcast state on the voyage home. As so often during his life, he felt keenly the lifelong isolation to which his peculiar vision had sentenced him, likening his present condition to the ridicule and scorn he had so long endured simply because he insisted that it was possible to do what no one else had: "I came to be, and I am, such that there is none so vile as not to dare to insult me."

An ailing and embittered Columbus rides back to Spain in chains in the hold of La Gorda *following his arrest on Hispaniola by Francisco de Bobadilla. He attributed most of his problems to the slanders of his enemies. "I declare that the violence of the evil speaking of disaffected persons has done me more injury than my service has profited me," he wrote to Ferdinand and Isabella.*

The High Voyage

Columbus's hurt at the injustice he believed had been done him knew no bounds. In a letter addressed to Juana de Torres, a governess in the royal household to whom both Columbus and Isabella were close, he poured out his feelings, scarcely able to believe that Isabella, who had supported him when no one else did, would now give credit to the slanders of his enemies. God had made him the "messenger" of the "new heaven and of the new earth," Columbus wrote, yet just because he had not brought back as much gold as people would have liked, he had been betrayed. He had been judged like a typical provincial governor, like one who had been sent to "Sicily or a city or two under settled government, and where the laws can be fully maintained, without fear of all being lost." About that, Columbus declared himself "greatly aggrieved," believing that he should have been judged "as a captain who went from Spain to the Indies to conquer a people, warlike and numerous, and with customs and beliefs very different from ours . . . and where, by the will of God, I have brought under the dominion of the king and queen, our sovereigns, another world, whereby Spain, which was called poor, is now most rich. I ought to be judged as a captain, who, for so long a time, down to this day, has borne arms, never laying them down for an hour." Despite this terrible turn of affairs, Columbus continued to repose

The loss of his privileges on Hispaniola left Columbus a greatly saddened man. He wrote Ferdinand and Isabella: "Of Española, Paria, and the other lands I never think without weeping. . . . I came to serve at the age of 28 years, and now I have not a hair on my body that is not grey, and my body is infirm, and whatever remained to me from those years of service has been spent and taken away from me and sold."

his trust in his God; he closed the missive by observing, "Our Lord God lives, with His power and wisdom, as in the past, and above all things he punishes ingratitude and wrongs."

Gloom now clung to Columbus, who seemed to embrace it as a kind of penance. The captain of *La Gorda*, the ship that returned the Columbus brothers to Spain, had offered to release the Admiral of the Ocean Sea from his chains, but Columbus had refused, stating that only his monarchs had the power to do so. At Seville, he took refuge in a monastery; the sight of the proud viceroy shuffling ashore in his frayed brown robe and fetters was said to greatly upset the town's populace, but Ferdinand and Isabella did not order his chains removed for another six weeks. Thereafter, Columbus always kept them with him and even stipulated that they accompany him to his grave.

Columbus met with his monarchs shortly before Christmas, 1500, at the Alhambra in Granada. Much had changed since their first encounter. Columbus was almost 50 years old, well past middle age by the standards of the

Columbus with Beatriz (far right) and his sons Diego (far left) and Ferdinand (center). Ferdinand sailed with his father on el alto viaje, *as the fourth voyage was known, and later became his biographer; his library of 15,000 volumes contained many of his father's books and papers.*

day, aged even more by the hardships he had endured. He moved slowly, hindered by severe rheumatism; when he bowed to honor his sovereigns, it was difficult for him to rise. Scars were visible on his wrists and ankles where the chains had bit into his skin. He remained loyal to the monarchs, but in the words of Las Casas, he now "loved them with a passionate hatred," angered at the disservice they had done him, grateful for their earlier support, hopeful that their faith could be rekindled. Isabella had also grown older and weary, burdened by the sorrow arising from the death, in young adulthood, of two of her children and the early indication of the madness that would blight the life of a third. She now, according to Andrés Bernáldez, a friend of Columbus's and one of Isabella's first biographers, "lived without joy." But the queen's heart had not been permanently hardened against the mysterious Genoan who had moved her so many years ago, and she treated him with a certain amount of solicitude.

In some respects, however, Columbus had not changed. He treated the monarchs to a tirade against Bobadilla that ended with a call for his execution. Columbus also demanded that all the rights, privileges, properties, and titles granted him by the Capitulations be restored. As was their wont, Ferdinand and Isabella told him they would think about it.

For nine months, Columbus fumed. He was well aware that for some time other explorers had been, in Las Casas's words, "encroaching on his islands." Pedro Alonso Niño, the former pilot of the *Santa María*, had discovered the mouth of the Amazon River. Alonso de Ojeda had somehow managed to obtain the map that Columbus had drawn of his third journey and had returned to the area of the Gulf of Paria. The Garden of Eden did not interest him, but the large numbers of pearls he found on the island of Margarita intrigued him no end, as they did Ferdinand and Isabella as well. Ojeda took with him another former

Portuguese mariner Vasco da Gama reached India in May 1497 by sailing around the Cape of Good Hope. The discovery of an eastern route to the Indies was more immediately momentous than any of Columbus's voyages; within six years of da Gama's expedition, spices in Lisbon were selling for only one-fifth of what they cost in Venice.

colleague of Columbus's, Juan de la Cosa, who drew a famous map of the expedition. Also along was Amerigo Vespucci, a witty and amusing Florentine who had long been in residence at the Spanish court. Vespucci's account of his adventures, which made no mention of Ojeda and was backdated two years, made him famous. On a second voyage that he made, in 1501, this time for Portugal, Vespucci ventured some 800 miles southward along the South American continent. During this same period another Genoan by birth, John Cabot, who sailed for England, discovered land far to the north, probably in present-day Newfoundland. Based on these new discoveries, a geographer named Duarte Pacheco Pereira speculated on the existence of a continuous land mass, a new continent, stretching from 70 degrees north latitude to 28 degrees south latitude.

For Columbus, accustomed as he was to thinking of Hispaniola as exclusively his, all these developments came as a further setback. It was as if he had been deprived not only of the personal possessions that Bobadilla had seized from him—his house, his books, his gold—but his intellectual property as well, for it was now clear that he had not found the Indies after all. That distinction belonged to Vasco da Gama, a Portuguese mariner, who in 1498 succeeded in reaching India using Dias's route around the Cape of Good Hope, thus making Portugal the most important power in Europe. After Columbus's death would come an even heavier blow to his prestige, as cosmographers took to calling the two New World continents "America," after Vespucci.

In September 1501, Ferdinand and Isabella reached their decision. Bobadilla would be recalled, but Columbus would not replace him. Nicolás de Ovando was named the new governor of Hispaniola; he would sail shortly at the head of a magnificent fleet of 33 vessels, at the command of 2,500 men. Columbus could retain his titles of viceroy and governor but none of his privileges; he was ordered to stay away from Hispaniola. An agent whom he trusted, Alonso de Carvajal, would be sent to attempt to obtain Columbus's gold for him. As compensation, the monarchs offered Columbus a very generous pension and a castle in Andalusia. He could live out the rest of his days in luxury, as befit a grandee of Spain.

The intrepid mariner could not be so easily bought off. He had a new idea. No one had yet explored the waters west of the Gulf of Paria; somewhere in that direction, he was now certain (as only Columbus could be certain), there must be a pass through which he could sail and still reach the Indies. Columbus was willing to concede the possibility that something lay between Europe and the eastern portion of Asia, but being unaware, like all Europeans, of the existence of the Pacific Ocean, he still believed that the Orient could not be far beyond the western lands that he had discovered. For months he hectored the monarchs,

Columbus's voyages enabled Spain to ultimately claim an enormous American empire, some of which can be seen on this early-16th-century Spanish map. After his death, Columbus was both criticized for introducing the institution of slavery to the New World and nominated for sainthood for bringing Christianity to the Americas.

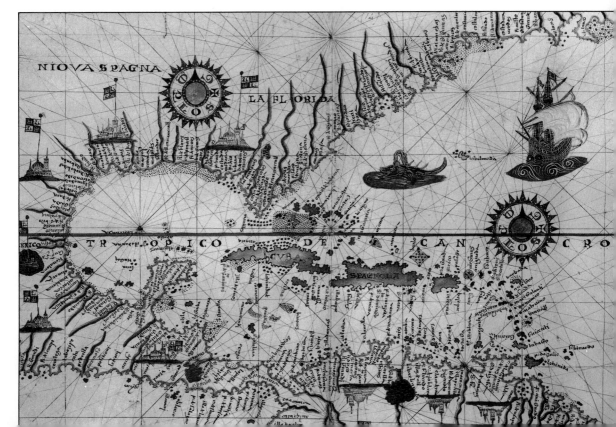

demanding that he be given some ships. Guilty over their treatment of him, eager to rid themselves of a disagreeable nuisance, they at last acquiesced. Columbus was given four small caravels and orders to stay away from Hispaniola.

Columbus's final journey—he always referred to it as *el alto viaje*, the high voyage—commenced at Seville on April 3, 1502. Many of the members of the crew were young boys between the ages of 12 and 18, among them Columbus's 12-year-old son, Ferdinand. Their commander seemed to them a strange and remote figure. He now claimed to navigate by dint of divine revelation, and his increasingly frequent periods of delirium only intensified his otherworldly air. Yet there was no doubt about his seamanship. The fleet reached the island of Martinique in 21 days, the fastest time across the Atlantic Columbus had made.

From Martinique, Columbus made for Hispaniola, in explicit defiance of his orders. Wanting nothing to do with the troublesome Genoan, Ovando denied him permission to land, but Columbus persisted, citing his need to replace an unsatisfactory ship and seek shelter from a hurricane that was brewing. The new governor scoffed at Columbus's pretense at soothsaying. Being new to the region and not as observant as Columbus, Ovando was not aware of the various atmospheric changes that portended a great storm, and he disregarded Columbus's recommendation that he hold in port a great fleet that was returning to Spain. The hurricane struck with a righteous vengeance, sending 25 of Ovando's ships to the ocean bottom. Among the passengers that were killed were Columbus's two great enemies, Bobadilla and Roldán; the only ship to make it to Spain was the nao carrying Columbus's gold, which Carvajal had succeeded in regaining for him. More fearful than ever of Columbus, whom he now regarded as something of a malign wizard, Ovando continued to refuse to allow him to land at Santo Domingo.

Frustrated, Columbus sailed in search of the strait. His fleet explored the coasts of present-day Honduras, Nicaragua, Costa Rica, and Panama without success. Bad weather followed them; at one point a storm tormented them for 28 consecutive days. Wrote Columbus:

> It was one continual rain, thunder and lightning. The ships lay exposed to the weather, with sails torn and anchors, rigging, cables, boats and many of the stores lost; the people exhausted and so down in the mouth that they were all the time making vows to go on pilgrimages and all that. . . . Other tempests I have seen, but none that lasted so long or so grim as this.

The exhausted Columbus was now all but broken in mind, unable to go ashore, reduced to giving orders from a doghouselike shelter his crew had rigged up for him on deck. His weakening body seemed to strengthen his spiritual side. At one point, according to the later testimony of a crew member, when a large funnel cloud was approaching the ships, he roused himself. Taking up a sword and the Bible, he declaimed loudly the story of Jesus walking on the Sea of Galilee and then traced a large cross in the sky. The cloud passed by harmlessly. On another occasion, while his men were engaged in a battle with Indians on shore, he climbed to the top of the foremast and howled wildly, until overcome by a vision in which the Lord reminded him of all that he had done for him—as much as he had done for Moses and David—and advised him to "fear not; have trust; all these tribulations are written upon marble and are not without cause."

Despite his perilous health, Columbus was desperate to press on, but the conditions of his ships, which were riddled with shipworms (clams that burrow into and eat away at submerged wood), forced him to head for Hispaniola. One ship had to be abandoned after the Indian battle; another sank on the way to Hispaniola, forcing the two remaining to head for Jamaica, the nearest island. On

Columbus wrote this letter to the Bank of Genoa in 1502 regarding the disposition of some property. His unusual signature reveals his sense of having been divinely chosen; a combination of Greek and Latin, pronounced Christoferens, it meant the Christ Bearer. The initials above his signature apparently stood for "Servant am I of the Most High Saviour, Christ Son of Mary."

June 25, 1503, Columbus ordered them run aground on a beach on Jamaica's southern coast.

There, Columbus and 115 members of his crew waited for more than a year to be rescued. The ships served as fortresses and living quarters; the local Indians were prevailed upon to provide the Europeans with food. When they balked at doing so after several months, Columbus, who was aware from an almanac that a lunar eclipse was scheduled, told them that his God was very angry with them and would demonstrate his displeasure on the last night of February. When the light of that evening's full moon was blotted out, the Indians grew terrified and promised to take care of the shipwrecked sailors so long as

Columbus on his deathbed. The Admiral of the Ocean Sea died unmourned by his adopted nation, which only later would realize the magnitude of the services he had provided it.

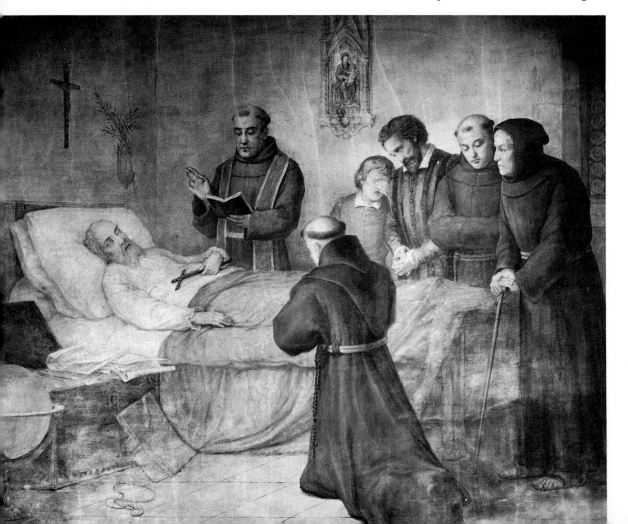

Columbus would speak to his Savior and have the moon restored. Thereafter, Columbus and his men were reasonably well fed. The ailing admiral managed to quell one final rebellion; finally, in June 1504, Diego Mendez and Bartholomeo Fieschi, who had made a heroic 108-mile canoe trip to Santo Domingo for help, persuaded Ovando to send a ship to Columbus's aid.

He made it back to Spain in November 1504. His final letter to his sovereigns reveals the depths of his exhaustion:

> Until now I have always taken pity on my fellow man; today, may heaven have mercy on me, may the earth cry for me, as I wait for death alone, sick and racked with pain. I am so far away from the Holy Sacraments that if my soul should here leave my body, not even God would remember it. Those who love charity, truth and justice, let them cry for me now.

There were few to cry for Columbus. Isabella was on her deathbed when he returned, and she died a few weeks later. Angered by Columbus's constant petitions to have his rights and privileges restored to his sons and heirs, Ferdinand would have nothing to do with him. Columbus's share of Hispaniola's gold made him fairly wealthy, but he could not forget all that he believed he had been cheated out of. Alone and bitter, barely able to move, Columbus spent his last years in rented houses in Seville, Segovia, and Valladolid, sustained by his old dream of mounting a crusade to free the Holy Land. He died in Valladolid on May 20, 1506. Except by those who were there with him—his two brothers, his two sons, and Mendez and Fieschi—his death went essentially unnoticed. Only a few mourners, none of them from the Spanish court, attended his funeral; as befit the remains of a fearless mariner, his body was moved several times before finding its final resting place, in the cathedral at Santo Domingo. It would not be until centuries later that Columbus attained the fame that his achievements warranted.

Further Reading

Boorstin, Daniel J. *The Discoverers: A History of Man's Search to Know His World and Himself.* New York: Random House, 1983.

Ceserani, Gian P. *Christopher Columbus.* New York: Random House, 1979.

Columbus, Ferdinand. *The Life of Admiral Christopher Columbus.* Translated and annotated by Benjamin Keen. New Brunswick, NJ: Rutgers University Press, 1959.

De Bry, Theodor. *Discovering the New World.* Edited by Michael Alexander. New York: Harper & Row, 1976.

Dolan, Sean J. *Christopher Columbus: The Intrepid Mariner.* New York: Ballantine, 1989.

Fernandez-Armesto, Felipe. *Columbus and the Conquest of the Impossible.* New York: Weidenfeld and Nicholson, 1974.

Goodnough, David. *Christopher Columbus.* New edition. Mahwah, NJ: Troll Associates, 1979.

Granzotto, Gianni. *Christopher Columbus: The Dream and the Obsession.* Translated by Stephen Sartarelli. New York: Doubleday, 1985.

Humble, Richard. *The Explorers: The Seafarers.* Alexandria, VA: Time-Life Books, 1978.

Irving, Washington. *The Life and Voyages of Christopher Columbus: To Which Are Added Those of His Companions.* Darby, PA: Darby Books, 1983.

Jane, Cecil, ed. *The Four Voyages of Christopher Columbus: A Documentary History.* New York: Dover, 1988.

Johnson, Spencer. *The Value of Curiosity: The Story of Christopher Columbus*. San Diego, CA: Oak Tree Publications, 1977.

McKendrick, Melveena. *Ferdinand and Isabella*. New York: Harper & Row, 1968.

Morison, Samuel Eliot. *Christopher Columbus, Mariner*. New York: New American Library, 1983.

————. *The Great Explorers: The European Discovery of America*. New York: Oxford University Press, 1978.

Newby, Eric. *The World Atlas of Exploration*. New York: Crescent Books, 1975.

Osborne, Mary P. *Christopher Columbus: Admiral of the Sea*. New York: Dell, 1987.

Skelton, R. A. *Explorers' Maps*. New York: Spring Books, 1958.

Soule, Gardner. *Christopher Columbus on the Green Sea of Darkness*. New York: Watts, 1988.

Stott, Ken. *Columbus and the Age of Exploration*. New York: Watts, 1988.

Chronology

Entries in roman type refer to events directly related to exploration and Columbus's life; entries in italics refer to important historical and cultural events of the era.

1416–60	Henry the Navigator presides over Portuguese exploration from his base at Sagres
1451	Christopher Columbus born Cristoforo Colombo in Genoa, Italy
1453	*Constantinople falls to the Ottoman Turks*
1455	Venetian navigator Alvise Ca'da Mosto explores the Senegal River for Portugal; *Johannes Gutenburg prints his famous Bible at Mainz*
1469	*Ferdinand of Aragon marries Isabella of Castile*
1470	Portuguese navigators discover the Gold Coast of West Africa
1472	*First edition of Dante's* Divine Comedy *printed*
1476	Columbus settles in Lisbon after surviving shipwreck off the coast of Portugal
1477	*Chaucer's* Canterbury Tales *published*
1478	*Spanish Inquisition begins*
1479	Columbus marries Felipa Perestrello e Moniz
1484–85	King João II of Portugal refuses to finance Columbus's proposed expedition to the Indies; Russians begin to explore Siberia; Portuguese navigator Diogo Cão reaches Cape Cross on Africa's west coast; Columbus leaves Portugal for Spain
1486–92	Columbus endures years of great anguish trying to convince Ferdinand and Isabella to sponsor his voyage

1488	Bartholomeu Dias rounds the Cape of Good Hope, opening an eastern route to the Indies for Portugal
1492	*The Moors surrender to Ferdinand and Isabella; Jews expelled from Spain*; Ferdinand and Isabella decide to finance Columbus's first voyage to the New World
Oct.–Dec. 1492	Columbus lands at San Salvador; goes on to discover Cuba and Hispaniola
1493–96	Second voyage of Columbus, in the course of which he discovers countless islands and firmly establishes the Spanish colony on Hispaniola; Henry VII of England commissions Venetian navigator John Cabot to discover a new trade route to Asia
1497–1500	Third voyage of Columbus; he discovers Trinidad and the continent of South America, but his heavy hand on Hispaniola brings about his arrest and return to Spain in chains; numerous Portuguese and Spanish voyages to the New World; Vasco da Gama of Portugal completes voyage to India
1502–4	Fourth and final voyage of Columbus
May 1506	Columbus dies in Valladolid, Spain

Index

Picture Credits

Stephen C. Dodge is a professor of history at Millikin University. He holds a Ph.D. from the University of Minnesota and has written extensively on the history of the West Indies.

William H. Goetzmann holds the Jack S. Blanton, Sr., Chair in History at the University of Texas at Austin, where he has taught for many years. The author of numerous works on American history and exploration, he won the 1967 Pulitzer and Parkman prizes for his *Exploration and Empire: The Role of the Explorer and Scientist in the Winning of the American West, 1800–1900*. With his son William N. Goetzmann, he coauthored *The West of the Imagination*, which received the Carr P. Collins Award in 1986 from the Texas Institute of Letters. His documentary television series of the same name received a blue ribbon in the history category at the American Film and Video Festival held in New York City in 1987. A recent work, *New Lands, New Men: America and the Second Great Age of Discovery*, was published in 1986 to much critical acclaim.

Michael Collins served as command module pilot on the *Apollo 11* space mission, which landed his colleagues Neil Armstrong and Buzz Aldrin on the moon. A graduate of the United States Military Academy, Collins was named an astronaut in 1963. In 1966 he piloted the *Gemini 10* mission, during which he became the third American to walk in space. The author of several books on space exploration, Collins was director of the Smithsonian Institution's National Air and Space Museum from 1971 to 1978 and is a recipient of the Presidential Medal of Freedom.